Folk High Schools in Bangladesh

*K.E. Bugge*

# Folk High Schools in Bangladesh

Translated from Danish

by

David Stoner

ODENSE UNIVERSITY PRESS
2001

The English edition has received economical support from N.F.S Grundtvigs Fond and from Landsdommer V. Gieses Legat

© K.E. Bugge and Odense University Press 2001

Printed by Narayana Press, Gylling, Denmark

ISBN 87-7838-572-5

Translated from Danish: K.E. Bugge »Folkehøjskoler i Bangladesh« by David Stoner

Cover illustration: Shapna, a former student of the school in Panchagram.

Where no other source is given, the photographs are by Ilse Bugge.

Odense Universitetsforlag
Campusvej 55
5230 Odense M

Tlf. 66 15 79 99
Fax 66 15 81 26
E-mail:Press@forlag.sdu.dk
www-location:www.oup.dk

# CONTENTS

FOREWORD  7

INTRODUCTION  9

BACKGROUND AND CONTEXT  11

A nation is born  11
The land and the water  14
The people and the culture  15
Religious traditions and counter-movements  15
Schooling and education  20

GONOBIDYALAYAS, SCHOOLS OF THE PEOPLE  23

External setting  23
Origins  24
Roots in the local tradition  27
Aims and objectives, hopes and intentions  28
The individual schools  32
　Khan Jahania (p. 32), Panchagram (p. 39), Central Gonobidyalaya (p. 40),
　Uchai (p. 43), Rangunia (p. 45)

SOME RELATED INITIATIVES  47

Protiggya Parishad (p. 47), MUL Center (p. 51), Santosh (p. 54)

LINKS WITH GRUNDTVIG  57

Folk high schools and Gonobidyalayas  57
　Context and further development (p. 57),
　Discovering the Originator (p. 60)

Development in the interpretation of Grundtvig  62
　A historical view,(p. 62) Popular enlightenment (p. 62), The school for life,
　(p. 65) Living interaction, (p. 67) Freedom (p. 69), New priorities (p. 75).

THE COMMOM AND THE PARTICULAR 77

Bangladesh, Denmark, and The Third World 77
The focus of the education 78
Human resources 79
> Education and the will to reform (p. 79), The importance of religion (p. 82), Gravity and humour (p. 85).

ABBREVIATIONS 86

INTERVIEWS 1998-1999 87

BIBLIOGRAPHY 88

# FOREWORD

It is most appropriate to start out here by extending my thanks to the institutions which, in a variety of ways, helped in the launching and carrying through of this project. The very first impulse came at the beginning of the 1990s from Dr Lilian Zøllner, then head of the research centre »Nornesalen« on the Danish island of Funen. Since then, the centre and its present leader, Thorstein Balle, have supported the work's completion. The Danish University of Education and the Democracy Fund have given grants for the study journeys that were made in 1998 and 1999. The Association of Folk High Schools in Denmark (FFD - Foreningen for Folkehøjskoler i Danmark) and the Danish Santal Mission have provided documentation and useful information. The Danish Educational Library has, with its usual efficiency, managed to procure books from distant libraries. And in Bangladesh itself the leadership and staff of the Bangladesh Association for Community Education (BACE) have given valuable help in arranging my study visits. I want to express my warmest thanks to these institutions for all this support and encouragement.

Next, I wish to thank the many individuals who have given me invaluable assistance over the past years. With her wide insight and personal commitment, Gunhild Skovmand Jensen of the International Committee of FFD has been a crucial help and inspiration throughout. For the understanding of the country's culture and recent history, two resource persons living in Bangladesh have been particularly important: the film-director and author Tanvir Mokammel and the historian Dr Ahmed A. Jamal of Dhaka University. Then, as so often before, my wife, Ilse Bugge, has given me excellent help in the choice of pictures and maps and with proof-reading. For all this support, which I have been given on the more personal level, I would like to express my hearty thanks.

Finally, my thoughts return to my meetings with a large number of people who are working in Bangladesh for the cause of popular education. One is both impressed and ashamed at witnessing how much these men and women - often in incredibly difficult circumstances - achieve for the benefit of the local community and the new nation. Their contribution has been and is great. This is still true, even though their names are known only within the narrow setting. But as has been said: »Great happenings happen silently«.

Vedbæk, May 2001                                                          K.E. Bugge.

# INTRODUCTION

This survey was originally planned as part of a series of publications whose *purpose* was to chart the spread of Grundtvig's educational views in countries outside Scandinavia. Since 1994 a conference report and five area studies have been published, after which the series came to an end in 1999. Although the present account is appearing as an independent publication, its purpose remains the same.

As regards the scope of this account, the spotlight is primarily directed upon the five folk high schools which are currently operating in Bangladesh and which, in the language of the country, are called »gonobidyalayas«. In addition, three schools are included which operate along similar lines although with different financing and backing organizations. Consequently the chronological aspect of the account centres upon the period from 1980 onwards, i.e. from the point when the first gonobidyalayas began their activities. However, this limitation does not exclude a broader perspective where this is deemed appropriate.

*The source material* consists of published and unpublished accounts including external and internal reports as well as interviews carried out during the above-mentioned study trips made in 1998 and 1999. These are supplemented by notes of conversations with the heads, teachers, and students of the schools. An unavoidable limitation has been that the written sources have been those which existed in either Danish or English. Also, to some extent interviews and conversations had to rely on the help of interpreters. It is therefore impossible to avoid misunderstandings completely, although efforts have been made to verify the information subsequently.

Two kinds of publications in particular enter the picture, when the question is raised as to how the present account relates to *earlier studies in this area*. If we consider accounts that describe and assess the gonobidyalaya projects as development projects, for instance reports available from DANIDA, the Danish development organization, we find that the overlap is minimal. We will find far more points of contact between the present account and the by now considerable amount of printed pamphlets and booklets that have been published since 1988 by the Association of Folk High Schools in Denmark. It is not surprising that this should be so. For within this association there has been much interest in what happens to Grundtvig's educational ideas from the moment they take root in cultural contexts remote from Danish soil.

Against this background, it will be apparent that in the following account there will be frequent references and reflections that are already well-known from publications of the Society. This account, however, differs from them in that it is a continuation of my own earlier studies, both the more theoretical overview of 1995, as well as my books on Canada from 1997 and 1999.

The account is arranged in four main sections. The first sketches in the essential background to the description of the high school initiatives that are in view here. Thus, the main geographical facts are mentioned, and particularly the significance of the historical roots for the development of the area's cultural distinctiveness. From the recent history of the country, those phases and events are outlined which are deemed to be particularly important in the present context. In conclusion, attention is drawn to the tasks and problems that present themselves within schooling and education.

The second section follows with a description of the Gonobidyalaya project. First, the administrative framework is sketched in, and some important events pertaining to the origins of the project are brought out. After a comparatively detailed treatment of the aims of the project, there is a concluding description of the individual folk high schools. Besides the five gonobidyalayas, three other institutions akin to them are presented, which however do differ from them in a number of points.

The third section aims first to identify some overriding characteristics in the development of the high school project described. After this, there are more specific reflections on the relation of the gonobidyalaya initiatives to the Danish highschool tradition, as well as to Grundtvig's ideas. The section is rounded off with a discussion of the contribution to Grundtvig interpretation that has emerged during this process.

The fourth and last section is concerned with the future. First, there is a reflection on the special conditions in Bangladesh that necessitate efforts within adult education. Then follows a discussion of the question of the central objective of such education. In conclusion, there is a review of the human resources that are available for such an initiative.

# BACKGROUND AND CONTEXT

*A nation is born*

Bangladesh is an unknown country to most West Europeans. This is probably because Bangladesh only impinges marginally - for instance in connection with natural disasters - on the attention of the western media. But even within its own local geographical setting of South Asia, Bangladesh occupies a marginal position in the north-eastern corner.

Even on a historical view, the area now called Bangladesh has not held any appreciable interest for Europeans. When the sea route between Europe and Asia was opened up around 1500 and onward, it was the markets of southern India, Indonesia and China which attracted attention. Throughout most of the following centuries the area was of interest to the British colonial masters only as the hinterland of the major city of Calcutta.

It was not until 1970-71, quite close to our own time, that Bangladesh seriously though briefly attracted the attention of the western media. The reason was the dramatic war of liberation that led to Bangladesh becoming an independent state. The historical factors behind this clash may be sought in a number of political decisions that were taken in relation to India's independence in 1947. During the years immediately preceding this, the joint organization of the Indian Muslims, the Muslim League, led by the influential lawyer *Muhammad Ali Jinnah* (1876-1948), had staked a claim for an independent Muslim state. Behind this demand was fear for the fate of Muslims in an independent India dominated by a considerable Hindu majority.

This was the reason behind the birth in 1947 of a new Muslim state called Pakistan, which embraced both the north-western provinces of former British India and the eastern part of the province of Bengal (see map). The two territories of this state were called West and East Pakistan.

This political construct was a surprise to most people. Few had had the fantasy to imagine a state consisting of two areas separated from each other by a distance of more than 1800 km. There were also profound differences of language, culture and business economics. The demand for the two to join up came from Jinnah's conviction that Pakistan would be unable to survive economically without the considerable tax revenues that could be levied in East Pakistan, whose popula-

*British India about 1930. In the east is Bengal with the provincial capital Calcutta. (Source: Brown 1985).*

tion throughout the period 1947-71 made up a majority of the joint state.

The fact that the vast majority of the populations of both East and West Pakistan are adherents of Islam was not sufficient to keep the two territories together in one state. The differences we have mentioned proved to weigh heavier in the long run. The Muslim League in its Lahore Declaration of 1940 had in fact already raised the possibility of establishing not one but two self-governing Muslim states of equal standing (Chowdury, p. 6; Baxter, 1984, p. 26).

The idea of an independent East Pakistan was thus soundly based. Against this background it is understandable that over the years the

*India and its neighbours about 1980. The eastern part of Bengal, which from 1947 until 1971 was called East Pakistan and formed a joint state with Pakistan, has now become an independent country called Bangladesh. (Source: Brown 1985).*

genuine contrasts became more acute until, in the spring of 1971, they were ignited in open rebellion. The violent fighting of the West Pakistani military against local nationalist groups as well as their atrocities against the civilian population of East Pakistan set off a stream of refugees to India. At one point their number reached some 10 million. With the aim of stopping this increasing flood of refugees, the Indian army intervened in the conflict. The West Pakistani military units in the area soon surrendered, and in December 1971 a new state was proclaimed with the name of Bangladesh.

The subsequent decades were politically troubled and marked by a series of bloody events. The one which attracted most attention in the western press was the murder of the leader of the struggle for independence, the country's first president, *Sheikh Mujibur Rahman* (1921-1975) and his family in August 1975. The following years brought continued unrest, military coups and periods of military rule and states of emergency. During the 1990s relative stability emerged. Democratic elections have been held, although personal and group interests still assert themselves to the detriment of new ideas and political institutions.

In connection with Bangladesh's obtaining of independence, there was debate as to whether this new nation would be economically viable. A frontier now separated the area from its natural market, which subsequently was in India. Another factor was that the conditions supplied by Nature were not unambiguously favourable.

## *The land and the water*

It has often been pointed out that Bangladesh is among the very poorest countries in the world. This is mainly due to overpopulation. Between 120 and 130 million people seek to survive in an area slightly larger than England. Despite a sizeable production of rice, it is necessary to import foodstuffs.

For the most part, Bangladesh consists of a spreading delta area in which two of the world's largest rivers, the Ganges and the Brahmaputra, flow into the sea. Every year, when the snow melts on the slopes of the Himalayas, the rivers burst their banks, creating huge floods. In addition, the rainfall in the mountainous border provinces to the north east exceeds the norm for the region. In summer months therefore a third of the country is under water. As if this were not enough, water also comes in from the south. From the Bay of Bengal, tidal waves some 5 to 7 metres high flow in across the flat terrain drowning people, animals and crops.

However, all this water is not just a constantly recurring plague, it is also a valuable resource. The country has plentiful drinking-water, something that in many Asian countries is more valuable than blood. The floods also deposit large amounts of fertile mud, which makes it possible to harvest not only two but in some parts three times a year. Finally, the rivers and their countless branches have since the dawn of time provided a fine mesh of traffic arteries. The ease of internal communication has always contributed largely to the cohesion of the country as a cultural unit. Just as in Scandinavia, the waterways have bound the populations closely together as regards language and outlook on life, whereas mountains and forests have tended to divide.

## The people and the culture

Under the British colonial administration, the province of *Bengal* formed an important administrative unit with Calcutta as its capital (see map). Over time, this populous province was divided several times into smaller units, most recently in connection with Indian independence in 1947. At that time, the eastern, largely Muslim, part of Bengal was separated off and joined to Pakistan as the eastern wing of this new state. As we have noted, the link with Pakistan ended in 1971, when Bangladesh was constituted as an independent state.

The name Bengal is usually traced back to a tribal group named Bang (Sanskrit: Vang), which formed part of the Indo-European immigration into India around 1500 BC. About 1000 BC this tribe seems to have reached the area nowadays called Bangladesh. The original population, of Dravidian or Mongol stock, was either absorbed or driven out into the border areas.

The language, Bangla or Bengali, spoken by almost 99% of the population, has been the official language of the country since the constitution of 1972. Bangladesh is actually the only country in South-east Asia that is almost 100% monolingual. The Bengali language has therefore become an integrating factor of inestimable significance. The language binds the various societal groups into one big community, thus crucially contributing to the development of a national identity.

Another important fact in this context is that there is a rich literary and poetic tradition in Bengali. Best known in the West is probably the writer and poet *Rabindranath Tagore* (1861-1941), who was awarded the Nobel Prize in 1913. This great poet wrote the national anthem of the country, »Sonar Bangla« (»Golden Bengal«). So it is hardly surprising that the people are proud of their culture and their language, which has become a symbol of their self-worth and independence. It is no coincidence that the very first postage stamp printed after the liberation of 1971 carries a picture of two students killed during a language dispute in 1952. The occasion was an attempt by the government in West Pakistan to impose Urdu as the official language.

Among the cultural factors that have shaped the self-awareness of the people are not only language, literature, and poetry, but also religion.

## Religious traditions and counter-movements

The mutual relations between religion and society can rarely, if ever, be described in static terms, as an arrangement fixed once for all and ever after functioning smoothly. This applies to Bangladesh. It is a clear illustration of how the relation between religion and society can, given the right conditions, change in character and develop in a surprising direction.

In 1947 the majority population's adherence to Islam had been the decisive argument for the then East Bengal (later Bangladesh) being joined with Pakistan in one state. In the period since Bangladesh in 1971 successfully fought for independence, Islam has continued to maintain its position as the religion of the great majority. According to Baxter (1984) and The Statesman's Yearbook (1999) it is estimated that in 1981 Muslims formed about 85% of the population and in 1997 88%. This background makes it necessary to take a closer look at the role played by religion in this society.

It is one thing to note the clearly dominant role of Islam. It is a different matter to make out how this position of power is administered. The interesting point emerges that Islam in Bangladesh, both traditionally and through most of the period of independence, has shown considerable tolerance to religious minorities. This observation does not fit in well with the dominant view in the West of Islam as a repressive religion - an impression that has been strengthened by developments in Iran after Khomeini's takeover in 1979.

Of the current factors that have helped to develop a remarkably tolerant version of Islam in Bangladesh, it would seem obvious to mention the significance of national cohesion that was created during the war of liberation. As might be expected, the struggle against a common external foe caused personal and ideological differences to fade into the background, at least for the first few years.

There is also another current factor. The essence of the newly won independence was indeed a break with a state in which a particular religion (in this case Islam) was the frame of reference; Islam was and is the foundational ideology under the constitution of Pakistan. This makes it understandable that through most of the 1970s the people of Bangladesh have shown great interest in the Indian model, according to which the state is secular. This is construed as the power of the state securing freedom of religion but not interfering otherwise in religious matters. The Bangladeshi constitution of 1972 describes the ideological basis of the new nation using phrases like »nationalism, socialism, democracy *and secularism* (our italics; cited in Baxter & Rahman, p. 123).

Beyond these causes shaped by the current situation lie deep historical roots in Bangladesh. We must first mention the strong Buddhist tradition which for some 1300 years was conspicuously influential and for the last 400 years of this period virtually functioned as the state religion. When, from the 13th century onward, *Buddhism* was first replaced by Hinduism and then by Islam as the majority religion, Buddhism continued to assert itself in the village population as an integrating factor and »peacemaker«. It is probably due to this ancient Buddhist tradition that the particular variant of Islam known as *Sufism* has become especially widespread in Bangladesh. One of the features shared by both Buddhism and Sufism is the significance attached to the individual's religious experience and to individual meditation.

The result of this development was an undogmatic mixed religion whose outward rites can be hard to categorize as regards their origin, but whose ethics place a high priority on non-violent behaviour and respect for the individual. In the country districts, where over 80% of the population still live, this religion has been handed down from generation to generation by wandering singers, known as Baul folk-singers, for instance the renowned Lalon (died 1890). Their cultural significance has been described as the most important element in Bengali literature of the 17th and 18th centuries (Walker I, pp. 129-130). In our time their texts and melodies have been studied, edited and commented upon by, among others, Tanvir Mokammel in 1996.

Last but not least, we must in this connection again point to the population's self-awareness and pride at being Bengalis. That this awareness is much more profound than any religious adherence was something that the founder of Pakistan, Muhammed Ali Jinnah, realized long ago. In an often quoted remark, he said that »a man is a Punjabi or a Bengali before he is a Hindu or a Moslem«. (Collins & Lapierre, p. 119). The question then was whether it would be possible for the Bangladeshis to maintain this tolerant version of Islam in the long run.

On the face of it, one might think that this tradition of tolerance, which not only had such deep historical roots, but had also been strengthened by dramatic current events, was so firmly in place that it was unshakeable. Nevertheless, shaken it was. The change of attitude was manifested in two areas: (1) From the end of the 1970s onward, the foundational ideology of the state was altered, so that Bangladesh became officially an Islamic state; (2) In 1990 and 1992 persecutions of the Hindu minority were witnessed.

## *On (1)*

In 1977, under President *Ziaur Rahman*, known as *Zia*, a constitutional change was carried out. The reference to secularization as a political ideal was then omitted. A new element was incorporated: that belief in Allah should hereafter be the basis for the whole activity of government (Ziring, pp. 127-128). This change raises the question of causes and consequences.

There were undoubtedly several causes. There may have been a wish to signal the country's own identity in relation to its large neighbour, India. People felt considerable distrust of India's Hindu majority and its government's secularizing religious policy. Also, there may have been a positive desire for rapprochement with the Islamic states, including obviously the rich Gulf states. Finally, we may point to the burgeoning fundamentalism of the 1970s, which was making itself felt in all parts of the world.

Initially, the consequences were not far-reaching. As we have emphasized, Zia's reforms gave Islam a »moderate prioritization« (Baxter, 1984, p 93). There was no question of introducing either religious compulsion or Islamic law. On the other hand, it may be said that the reform gave Islam an official preferential position. At the end of the 1980s, under President *H.M. Ershad*, the process of Islamization was accentuated. It then became customary for leading figures of the state to attend Friday prayers and major Muslim festivals. For instance, Prime Minister *Sheikh Hasina* attended the Ijtema Pilgrimage which was held a little north of Dhaka in February 1999 . Finally, over the last few years the state has given considerable grants to Muslim institutions. In the longer term, it was inevitable that, for instance in the armed forces and among orthodox Islamic theologians, there would be a wish for a clearer stress on Islam's new status and a more restrictive interpretation of Islam. However, to our knowledge no definite steps have been taken in this direction.

## On (2)

In 1990 events in India were to have gruesome repercussions in Bangladesh. We refer to what was known as the *Ayodhya* case, after a town in northern India. It has been asserted, but never proved, that about 450 years ago a mosque was erected on a site where a Hindu temple had once stood. In the autumn of 1989, an extreme right-wing Hindu party held an inauguration ceremony at this spot as the first step towards »re-erecting« a Hindu temple on the disputed site. As might be expected, this initiative gave rise to waves of violent clashes continuing into 1990, in which thousands of Hindus and Muslims lost their lives. The disturbances reached new heights when, on 6 December 1992, militant Hindus pulled down the mosque.

The Hindu fanatics who carried out the demolition probably did not give it a thought that this action might be expected to spark off violent reprisals against Hindu minorities in neighbouring Islamic countries, including Bangladesh. But that is what happened in both 1990 and

1992. In her much discussed book »Shame«, the Bangladeshi author Taslima Nasrin has written about several hundred cases of attacks on Hindus and the looting and burning of temples. The immediate and violent reactions in Bangladesh are said to have been sparked off when the TV reports of the dramatic events in Ayodyha were immediately transmitted to the remotest corners of Bangladesh.

Taslima Nasrin's book is a fictional account of one Hindu family's fate during these disturbances. To highlight the situation, she has inserted into her narrative a number of documentary accounts of the violent episodes, which are recorded with exact times and places. In her foreword, the author tells us that, to the best of her ability, she has verified the data. This reservation on her part might cause us to be a little sceptical about the reliability of the material. In any event, the accounts, filling 22 closely printed pages, make a deep impression. And it is a fact that the Hindu percentage of the Bangladeshi population has declined from 13.5% in 1974 to 10.5% in 1991 (Baxter 1984, p. 92; 1996, p. 92).

In spite of political reforms and spontaneous religious revenge attacks, which in some places also affected other minority groups than Hindus, the tradition of tolerance seems to have survived. The constitutional reform of 1977 was cautious and limited. And the accent on religion at the end of the 1980s did not bring any major changes. Ershad's initiative was met with scepticism and open criticism. A secular attitude to life was and is far more widespread than might be suspected in an officially Islamic society. In this context it is thought-provoking that a book professing a rationalistic secular view of life (Matubbar, 1988) should be published at this very time.

The crucial factor contributing to the survival of tolerance is probably that intolerant one-sidedness is in basic conflict with Bengali national identity. This is probably where we should seek the reason why there have been no systematic campaigns of extermination against religious minorities in Bangladesh as there have been against the Bahais in Iran. Nor has the Islamic penal code been introduced, as in Saudi Arabia.

In the years since 1992 there have been no reports of any violent episodes approaching those of 1990 and 1992. So there is no question of the tradition of tolerance being replaced by a new and aggressive basic attitude. Rather, these events were limited episodes of violence reacting to concrete events at the time. What they have shown, however, is that no tradition is unshakeable. At some point, all traditions will be challenged by a new situation. The question is whether the tradition is capable of renewing itself.

## Schooling and education

In *pre-colonial Bangladesh*, which was more or less a traditional Islamic society, schooling normally took place in the mosques. The aim was to impart the literacy that was necessary for reading the Koran. In addition, there was practical instruction in the rituals performed during Friday prayers and at the regularly recurring festivals.

Teaching could also take place elsewhere, for instance as part of the training which both princely courts and business houses found it necessary to set up for their young employees. In contrast to the stability and predictability that marked the instruction in the mosques, these educational activities were marked by changing content and fairly casual organisational forms. However, it is important to underline that even in *pre-colonial* society, there was teaching whose scope and significance should not be underestimated.

During the *colonial period*, the new governors had an understandable interest in training an indigenous elite able to serve in the administration. For this, schools and colleges were set up. Another method, often preferred, was to give grants to private institutions.

The schools and educational centres of colonial times were organized on European lines. The content of the teaching was shaped by what was deemed necessary with a view to carrying out administrative functions. Furthermore, mastery of English and the acquisition of »civilized« behaviour and thinking was required. The schools aimed at the restricted number of young people who were interested in an office training. On this point, these schools differed from the mosques, where teaching was offered to all children of believing parents.

On achieving independence in 1971, *the new state of Bangladesh* inherited an outdated and unpractical school system. The time was past for a narrow, elitist system. What was needed was a broadly based positive activation of the masses, i.e. an unlocking of the enormous potential represented by the 100 million inhabitants of the state. The new times also called for new knowledge and new skills. It may be added that a population living largely on the verge of starvation needs knowledge and skills that can fairly quickly be turned into improvements in the individual's conditions. But before a new schooling can be introduced it is necessary for the elementary basics to be in place. This is where the question of literacy comes into the picture.

In two reports issued by UNESCO, one in 1984 and one in 1985, the percentage of readers in 21 Asiatic developing countries has been assessed (LSAP, 1984 and 1985). These reports show that Bangladesh is among the seven countries in which literacy is lowest, i.e. below 50%.

According to the Bangladeshi census of 1974, literacy was then as low as 22.2%. The reports also showed that a low literacy rate in these countries is accompanied by a number of other socio-economic factors that hamper development, e.g. hunger and malnutrition, the prevalence of infectious diseases, high infant mortality etc.

Even before 1971, the government of the joint state of Pakistan initiated an adult education programme aimed at increasing literacy. However, it had little effect, partly due to its limited scope, partly because no opportunities were created for maintaining the newly gained literacy.

Since independence, the government and other authorities have taken a number of different initiatives for the teaching of both children and adults. They wanted to make a start in keeping the promise that had been made in § 17 of the Constitution, which says that it shall be a basic principle of the State's educational policy »that a uniform, mass-oriented and universal educational system be set up and that free and compulsory education be given to all children at the ages which are to be laid down by law.« (quoted Ali, 1995, p. 70).

This declaration is clearly divided into two parts separated by »and that«. The first part deals with what applies generally, see the word »universal«, which in principle includes both adults and children but which with the choice of the term »mass-oriented« presumably chiefly has the adult part of the population in view. The second part unambiguously deals with children.

In 1973, in order to secure the education of the youngest children, all private primary schools, which in Bangladesh cover years 1-5, were nationalized. About 5000 new schools were built and an intensive teacher-training drive was commenced. Even by about 1980, however, it was evident that these initiatives had begun to crumble. Linda Dove (1981) mentions as the main causes:
– that about half the children enrolled never go to school
– that about 3/4 of the pupils do not complete their schooling (»dropouts«)
– that to an unforeseen extent the teachers do not turn up to teach (»teacher absenteeism«)

Another factor is the lack of resources for obtaining materials.

Among other new initiatives, the most remarkable are those within *adult education*. »Mass education« was not only mentioned in the Constitution but also in the country's second five-year plan (1980-85) as an area of top priority. In this field, the authorities have collaborated extensively with private and with overseas organizations. Among these, we can pick out the large-scale »Mass Education Programme« (MEP) set up in collaboration with the Danish development agency DANIDA back in 1978/9. The project, which was localized in the Noakhali district in the south of the country, was integrated in a number of other aid projects aimed at developing agriculture and small industries as well as improving health and infrastructure. However, here too the apparently insuperable difficulty has been encountered of how to maintain literacy once it has been acquired. Another difficulty of the MEP project was that there were several different views about how »integration« was to be understood.

There can be no doubt that these initiatives for children and adults have had a favourable effect. A statistic from 1996 states that the literacy rate has now risen to 44.8% (Jamal, Annex 4), a doubling in comparison to the rate of 1974 mentioned above. Nevertheless, there is a long way still to go. There was therefore great interest in trying out the new opportunities that came along in the early 1980s. At that time, the folkhighschool idea was introduced into Bangladesh. The question now was how far these new schools could not only help to increase literacy, but also contribute to a general improvement in the conditions of the population.

# GONOBIDYALAYAS, SCHOOLS OF THE PEOPLE

*External setting*

In the post-war period, several different types of adult education were set up in Bangladesh. The impulses came from domestic as well as overseas organizations. An early example of the latter is the Noakhali project already mentioned, in which the teaching of children and adults was integrated. Currently, over 300 aid projects are ongoing in Bangladesh, and several of them include an element of adult education. The projects linked with the Danish folk high school tradition are therefore by no means alone in the field.

The centres of adult education inspired by the Danish high-school idea are called Gonobidyalas, i.e. »schools of the people«. Gono means »people« and bidyalaya »school«. At the time of writing, in spring 2000, five of these schools are operating. One is located near the capital Dhaka. Three are located north, west, and south of the central school. A fourth is rather isolated, in the mountainous south-eastern region bordering upon Burma, nowadays called Myanmar (see map).

All five schools operate to a shared set of rules. Each school has a norm of 60 students divided roughly equally between the sexes. The age range is from 15 to 25. Usually 3-5 teachers as well as an accounts clerk are employed at every school. Each school is headed by a principal. There is local supervision by a committee, known as the General Council, whose members reside in the area. The overarching control rests with a countrywide association with an office in Dhaka. This is a private organization, the Bangladesh Association for Community Education, abbreviated to BACE. As this title suggests, BACE sees it as its task to promote »community education«, i.e. educational activities out in the various local communities. In October 1981 BACE concluded an aid agreement with the Danish agency DANIDA. Some years later, in 1988, the role of Danish partner was taken over by Foreningen af Folkehøjskoler i Danmark (the Association of Folk High Schools in Denmark) known as FFD. BACE and FFD jointly undertake administrative and educational responsibilities. By far the greater part of the schools' financial base is in the form of grants from Denmark. And right from the autumn of 1980, just before the formalized collaboration became a reality, the Danish high-school idea has been an important factor in the way the schools' teaching has been organized.

In accounts of the activities of the gonobidyalayas the term *non-formal education* is often used. According to recent educational definitions (e.g. Holck, 1995; Ehlers, 2000), this term refers to any teaching which is »not formal« in the following respects. There are no definite admission requirements; there are no formalized examination requirements and, consequently, a fair amount of freedom in arranging the teaching. The emphasis is on the acquisition of skills. The entry qualifications of students and teachers are not usually officially stipulated, but there are provisional and flexible guidelines.

## Origins

It is not possible to give a complete history of the origins of these schools. A number of details such as exact dates and the scope and scale of previous local initiatives are difficult to verify. However, by supplementing existing written accounts with oral information, it is possible to establish a number of facts.

Among the main factors present in the immediately preceding decade we must mention what is known as the *Swarnivar movement*, which has been a presence in the country districts from 1974/75 onward, but has roots much farther back. Swarnivar means »self-help«. Thus, there is a parallel with the movements which arose at the end of the 1960s in other third-world countries with the aim of promoting »self-reliance«. In Bangladesh the movement was organized on the local level under the leadership of broadly composed village committees. A characteristic slogan ran: »Let beggars' hands become working hands!« (Baxter & Rahman, p 153).

In 1975, in Rangunia north-east of Chittagong, an NGO was set up, which was named »*Swarnivar Bangladesh*, i.e. a self-helped Bangladesh. The aim of the organization, whose leader was the former government official *Mahabub Alam Chashi*, was to help impoverished countryfolk to be self-reliant. To achieve this, it was necessary for them to acquire the knowledge and skills required both to make a co-operative movement operational and, indeed, generally to achieve new earnings potential. On Mr Chashi's initiative, a training centre was set up for the population groups attached to the movement. For the erection of the centre, support was received from several sources. The site was made available by private individuals and public authorities, and the local population gave their labour and building-materials without charge.

During the same period, 1975-80, two similar projects were set in hand. One of these ran in the village of Uchai, about 450 km north-west of Dhaka. The initiator in this case was a village doctor called *Dr Rustam Ali*. His institution was called Gonobiswabidyalaya to emphasize that it was a university of the people. »Biswabidyalaya« means university.

The other school project proceeded in Panchagram near Comilla. Here, in close partnership with a local co-operative, education of poor adults from the area was started up. The initiator here was the socially concerned official *Dr Abdus Sattar*, who was chairman of BACE and also a friend and former colleague of Mr Chashi mentioned above. During a study trip to Europe, Dr Sattar had come to know Danish folk high schools. It is not possible to give a precise date, but at some time at the end of the 1970s he decided that the teaching at Panchagram should be patterned upon the Danish folk high schools.

On *15 September 1980* in Panchagram *the first gonobidyalaya* was opened under BACE's auspices. Among the far-reaching perspectives in this event, there may be particular reasons for spotlighting the following:

- that by being linked to a smoothly operating and country-wide organization the local initiative acquires a stronger and broader foundation
- that the choice of the term *gonobidyalaya*, »school of the people«, not only suggests an association with the folk-high-school idea, but also conveys a clearly anti-elitist educational policy.
- that either on the same occasion or very shortly afterwards it was decided to set up four similar schools in other districts.

In the course of events outlined here, Dr Sattar's particular background and educational interests have played a vital role. But at an early stage there was a more direct influence from Denmark and the Danish folk high school. This is how it came about: In the late 1970s Daniel Pedersen, as educational adviser for DANIDA, was attached to the Danish embassy in Dhaka. In that capacity he made contact with BACE, which was set up in 1977. In 1977, in fact, Daniel Pedersen gave a lecture at BACE about Danish folk high schools. He has given the following account of the lecture:

> I came and told them about the background to the Danish high schools and about Denmark's situation at that time, which in so very many areas resembles the situation in Bangladesh today: people were illiterate, they were dying of cholera and tuberculosis, and Denmark was bankrupt after the Napoleonic wards. We chatted about the possibility

of doing something similar in Bangladesh. (Hamre 1994b, p. 39).

In August 1981, against the background of developments in 1975-80, BACE, in partnership with Daniel Pedersen, applied to DANIDA for financial support. The application makes it clear that in its original form the 1981 partnership project consisted of the following:

- the aim of further developing five existing adult education centres-besides Panchagram, one in each of the country's four other main districts.
- the intention that these five schools should act as some kind of models (»model gonobidyalayas«) for about 200 other centres.
- the intention of appealing to marginal social groups, mainly children, women, small peasants, and workers.
- that the centres should accept BACE as the co-ordinating organization.
- that it was originally envisaged that the students should live in at the schools, and that therefore a hall of residence should be built at each school with accommodation for 60 students.

These points make it clear that it was not intended to transfer Danish folk high schools lock, stock and barrel to Bangladesh. This is also plain from the caution in Daniel Pedersen's phrase »something similar«. What was desired was to use the high-school idea as an inspiration for already ongoing school projects, i.e. the initiatives which BACE was already co-ordinating. It was also emphasized that it was desired that the schools should incorporate small workshops, agricultural education, and training in relevant practical skills. Teaching aimed at enhancing the students' earnings potential was unknown in Danish folk high schools, or offered only to a very limited degree.

Based upon the aid agreement of October 1981, the first grants were given by DANIDA. We have seen that originally five schools were envisaged. One school project was soon abandoned (see below), but in the end a fifth school was set up some years later. As regards the centre in Rangunia mentioned above, it proved to be of importance that Mr Chashi was a member of BACE's board. He was either present himself at Daniel Pedersen's lecture in 1977 or heard about it soon after from the chairman of BACE, Dr Abdus Sattar. However that may be, in 1981 Mr Chashi proposed that the centre in Rangunia should also become part of the new partnership with Denmark which BACE was then in the process of formalizing. This was quickly agreed.

## Roots in the local tradition

With the soil so well prepared by the potential of the gonobidyalaya project's immediate past, it took a relatively short time, about five years, for a remarkable fusion to take place between local initiatives and ideas from outside, including Denmark. However, it gradually became apparent that events were also being driven along by sources of inspiration which are not given so much attention in daily life, but which do make their influence felt. We are thinking of concepts and ideas from the Bengali cultural tradition and from neighbouring India.

A number of interesting points about the *adult education* practised in Bangladesh even *prior to 1981* are made by Tanvir Mokammel & Abdul Gofur, in their monograph »Gonobidyalaya. School for Life« (1991/2). They cite a number of examples showing that »non-formal« adult education has roots going back a long way in the people's own tradition. They first mention two Bengali cultural figures, *Ishwarchandra Vidyasagar* (1820-1891), and *Rabindranath Tagore* and his famous school Shantiniketan. Both these writers made a considerable contribution for the benefit of oppressed groups in society. As representatives of a tradition that is common to the whole sub-continent, Mokammel and Gofur mention first *Mahatma Gandhi* and then the institution Mitraniketan in South India that was inspired by Gandhi. Finally they mention two types of Indian schools called Ashram and Tol; these are jointly characterized as »residential educational institutions« (p. 3).

Whereas Tagore and Gandhi are well-known names in Europe, the other names and terms will need some explanation. Ishwarchandra Vidyasagar lived and worked in Calcutta, where in 1850-58 he was the principal of Sanskrit College there. He also initiated social reforms, for instance of widows' rights within Hinduism, as well as working hard for the education of women (Tripathi, chap. V). His involvement in schools and education are evidenced both by his publication of a number of popular textbooks and by the fact that it was he who conducted the official opening of a new institution for teacher-training in Calcutta in July 1855 (Mukerji II, p. 309).

*Mitraniketan* is the name of an institution in South India which is chiefly engaged in adult education. This institution, founded in 1956 and now headed up by K. Viswanathan, was described in detail in the book published by Jeff Biggers in 1996. An *ashram* is the place where a guru lives with and instructs his disciples. The word *tol* means a boarding-school where there is instruction in Sanskrit (Walker I, pp. 320-322).

## Aims and objectives, hopes and intentions

The gonobidyalaya project had now been launched. In that situation it was vital to set out clearly the course along which it was to sail. In other words: what were its aims? In a manuscript of 1817 Grundtvig himself emphasized that such clarifications are important (Bugge, 1965, p. 211). Of recent years, with the emphasis on curriculum development that has arisen since the Second World War, intensive work has been done on formulating and systematizing educational objectives. This interest in setting out objectives still continues.

It is characteristic of the gonobidyalaya project that from the very beginning great care has been shown to formulate clear educational objectives. It is also true that over the past twenty years the objectives have from time to time been adjusted and reformulated. In the following, we shall focus upon three representative texts which will be quoted and commented upon in chronological order. Other texts which exist in draft form, in applications and pamphlets etc. will supplement these statements, but bring no important corrections.

The oldest statement of aims is found in the application from BACE which we have mentioned, submitted in August 1981, a text that has been quoted and summarized by Uffe Geertsen in the last of his four articles of 1983. The relevant paragraphs run:

> The objective of the centres is to support and further develop five adult education centres (Gonobidyalayas) that will act as models for about 200 similar centres elsewhere in Bangladesh. The purpose of the centres is to involve the poor rural population in development work through vocational and social education (p. 1). The centres target in particular marginal groups such as children, women, small peasants, and workers. (p. 2).

First, the *background* and *future perspectives* are sketched in. It is stressed that the gonobidyalayas are not planned, they are already existing centres for adult education (note: »support and further develop«). Then the setting up of about 200 similar schools is mentioned. This is probably an expression of a realistic assessment of the number of schools required if they are to have any appreciable impact on the population as a whole. The idea of these 200 schools seems to have been abandoned later, however.

The *target groups*, i.e the clientele for whom the new schools are intended, are detailed. It is the part of the rural population who find it hardest to make their views known - and hardest to improve their lot.

These groups are now to be brought into »development work«. It may surprise us that in this context children are also in view. This is perhaps because children were already integrated into the Noakhali project (see above). The »workers« mentioned at the end must in this context be rural workers.

For development to take place, the people concerned must be offered »vocational and social education«. In other words the students must be enabled to improve their economic situation, and in addition they must be equipped to be able to utilize their social and political opportunities in society. This societal education is probably the closest we get here to the Danish folk-high-school idea, which is not specifically mentioned.

The next statement of aims, which describes the second phase of the project, is found in a report of 1994, i.e. six years after FFD had entered into a collaboration with BACE. Chapter five of the report deals with Objectives among other things. We quote from it:

> 5.2.1 *Overall Objectives*. The overall objectives of the Gonobidyalaya Project are: to provide low-cost, non-formal education to the poorest segments of the rural population with little or no education, in order to improve their standard of living; and to act as a centre of inspiration for social development based on the concept of the Danish Folk High School Movement.
>
> 5.2.2 *Immediate Objectives of the Gonobidyalayas*. The immediate objectives are: to improve the students' understanding of life and society and upgrade their literary proficiency; and to improve students' skills in order to improve their living conditions through production and income-generating activities. (Final Report. Mid-term review, p. 22).

Initially, we note that the headings contain some unclear language. As »overall« here refers to the highest level in the hierarchy of objectives, one might have expected »subordinate« or »specific« as the lower level. Also, in contrast to »immediate« one might have expected »remote«, either in time or place.

*The first paragraph*, which describes the overall objectives, is divided into two sections by a semicolon. In the first section, »to improve their standard of living« counts as the highest objective; the »non-formal education« mentioned at the start describes the subordinate objective whose achievement is to serve the overall objective, the improvement of their living conditions. The second paragraphs lays down as the overall objective that the gonobidyalayas are to be capable of acting as an inspiration to social development. It is then added that this formulation builds upon the Danish folk-high-school idea.

Thus, the overall objectives are clearly and unambiguously described in economic and social terms (»standard of living... social development«). We note as an oddity that in a prominent place in the statement, the first requirement mentioned is that the education aimed at must be »low-cost«. Such expressions are to be expected in budgets, not statements of objectives. The expression is omitted from later documents.

*The second paragraph*, too, is divided into two sections by a semicolon. In the first section we find two well-known educational objectives: »understanding ... proficiency.« It is emphasized that the aim is not to impart this understanding and proficiency to the students. It is to »improve and upgrade« what they have already taken on board. We also note that the use of the expression »understanding of life« must refer to the Danish high-school tradition. It is not an expression we normally expect to find in the context of development aid.

In the second section, the word »improve« occurs twice. Otherwise the section is dominated by economic terms (»living conditions...production...income«). However, it is worth noting that the high-school idea is found in both paragraphs.

The most recent statement is contained in an address given by *Dr Ahmed A. Jamal* in March 1998. Thus, even though the statement was not issued by the leadership itself, but is found in a lecture about these schools, the principles it sets out are of interest.

> 3.2 The GB Concept. Inspired by Grundtvig's idea of *enlightenment* of the people through an *education for life*, the GB Concept envisages conscientisation and empowerment of the most vulnerable section of the rural youth in Bangladesh through a life-oriented education. The Concept centres around the idea of human development, which implies development of human qualities and skills among people who need them most, and thereby transform them from »passive victims of enforced development« (Danish Draft Policy paper, 1996) to active participants in social progress. (Jamal, p.6).

Dr Jamal's pithy formulation starts out from the inspiration of Grundtvig's thinking on popular enlightenment and a school for life. Then, straight away, the key concepts of »conscientisation« and »empowerment« are brought in. We note that the first section of the statement, up to the first full stop, has a parallel structure. Just as Grundtvig wished to bring about popular *enlightenment* of the people using a school for life, in the same way those within the gonobidyalaya project wish, according to Dr Jamal, to create *conscientisation and empowerment* of rural youth through a life-oriented education.

The expressions »conscientisation« and »empowerment« have been taken from the Brazilian educationist *Paulo Freire* (born 1921), whose ideas have exerted a radical influence on recent educational thinking in the Third World. In his address Dr Jamal makes several references to Freire.

The link between Grundtvig and Freire, between the folk high schools and the gonobidyalayas, is seen in the quoted statement of objectives and in the clear interest seen in the lecture in human beings and what is human, i.e in a humane development. The stressing of this objective could not but lead to a high priority being given to an education that promotes the development of human »qualities and skills«. And the broader result that is expected and hoped for, is set out in terms inspired by Freire. It is true that the word »*emancipation*« is not actually mentioned, but the idea is very much present. Partly referring to an original Danish formulation, it is stressed that the desired human development will transform the students from »passive victims of enforced development« to active participants in social progress, in other words emancipation.

The conscious activation of the students in the learning process, which is stressed so much here, once again represents a point on which the thoughts of Grundtvig and Freire meet. On the first page of Dr Jamal's lecture, we find a third point. Here, Freire's thoughts about a dialogue-based education is put alongside Grundtvig's ideas about the decisive importance of conversation for education and social life. Back in 1978 Sven Borgen drew attention to this similarity between Freire's thinking and Grundtvig's words about a »living interaction«. For obvious reasons Dr Jamal had no knowledge of this article, which was written in Danish.

## Summary

The statements of objectives we have cited and commented upon differ in their scope, structure, and degree of detail. However, they are united in stressing that the poorest inhabitants of rural districts should be the primary target group of the gonobidyalaya project. They are also united in pointing to the desirability of an education that aims to change attitudes as well as impart skills.

Then, we note that none of the three formulations have been structured according to the classic curriculum theory whereby educational objectives are categorized in three groups according to whether they deal with knowledge, skills or attitudes. However, the realities behind these terms are certainly covered both directly and indirectly. The use of a tight schematization might indeed have seemed artificial and uninspiring.

Finally, in these three formulations we can detect some lines of development. Over the 15 years covered by them we note an increasing fascination with the high-school idea and with Grundtvig's thoughts. In the last of the three texts, Grundtvig is not only mentioned by name and quoted, his thoughts are even placed in a current international context. In other words, we find an appropriation of Grundtvig's ideas which discusses them and places them in perspective.

In conclusion, we must recall the sober acknowledgement expressed in the third of Uffe Geertsen's articles of 1983: »One thing is sure. There is a very great distance between the wished-for world of the project-describers and the reality we - in part - encountered.« And here too, there is a great distance between the statements of objectives we have cited and the harsh reality of rural life in Bangladesh. On the other hand, it must be borne in mind that without the visions that lie behind the statements of objectives, no progress will be made.

## The individual schools

Against the background of the account we have just given of some of the overall features common to the Gonobidyalaya project, we shall now make some more specific observations about the individual schools. These descriptions are based on printed and written materials which make mention of the schools, as well as on my own notes from visits made to the schools in 1998 and 1999.

## Khan Jahania Gonobidyalaya

This school is in the south-western corner of the country, a few kilometres west of the town of Bagerhat and about 80 km from the Indian frontier. The very name of the school manifests its deep roots in the history of the area. *Khan Jahan* (died 1459), also called Khan Jahan Ali, was a Muslim prince who ruled in the area in the mid-fifteenth century. During his reign, Khan Jahan, who belonged to the Sufi sect of Islam, manifested an unusual organizational talent combined with a concern for the welfare of his people. Not only did he build large reservoirs for collecting drinking-water for his people; he also built so many mosques

## Bangladesh

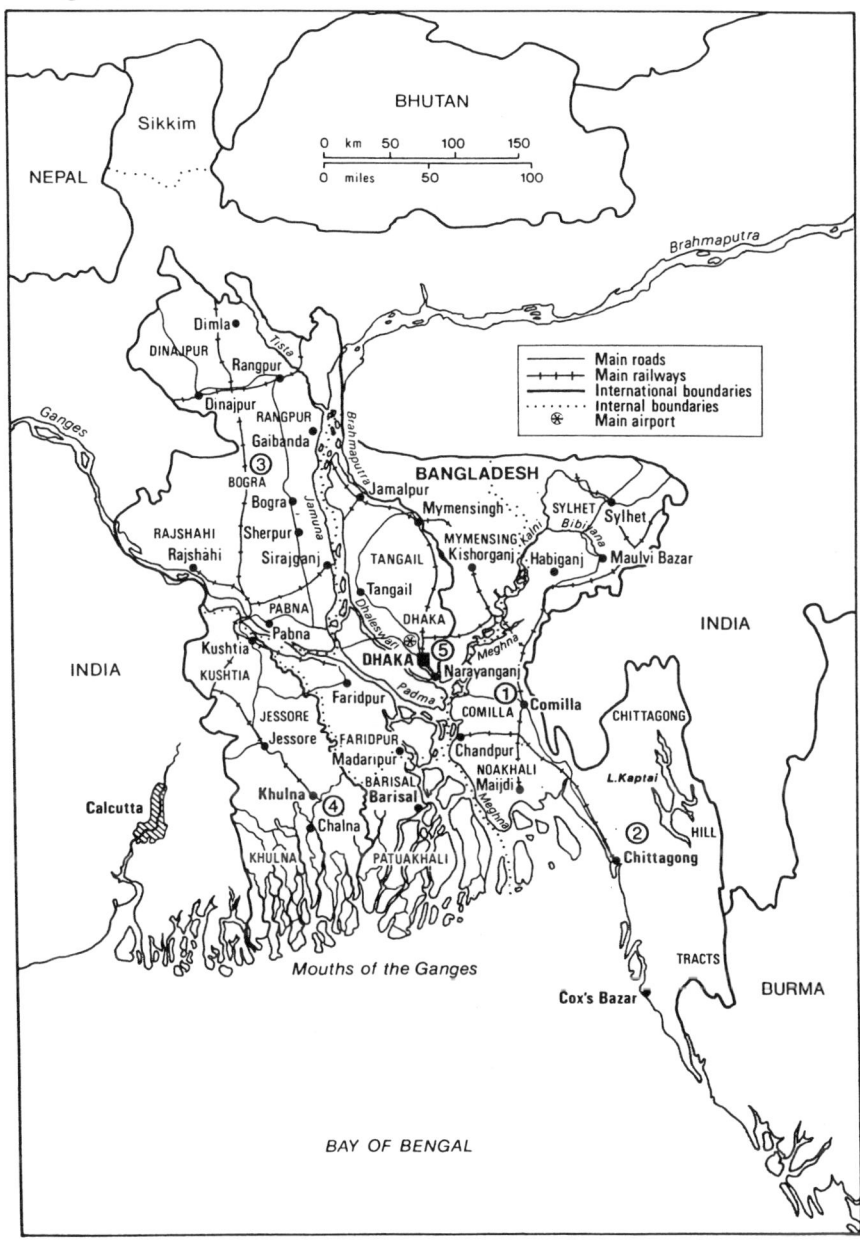

1. Panchagram Gonobidyalaya
2. Rangunia Gonobidyalaya
3. Uchai Gonobidyalaya
4. Khan Jahania Gonobidyalaya
5. Sonargaon Central Gonobidyalaya (under construction)

*The geographical location of the five folk high schools, which are known as gonobidyalayas in the language of the country. (Source: BACE/FFD)* that the number of them is exceeded only by the mosques of the capital Dhaka. Some of the buildings which Khan had erected still rank among the country's most renowned monuments. Among them is usually reckoned the great mosque with 60 domes (actually 77). It is no wonder that the people of the region are proud of this prince, who is regarded almost as a saint. It is no coincidence that the songbook used at Khan Jahania Gonobidyalaya has a picture of the 60-domed mosque on the cover.

The structure and content of the teaching follows the same pattern as at the other gonobidyalayas. After morning assembly, the principal, teachers, and students discuss the allotment of the practical work, in which all participate and which in Bengali is called »*shramdan*«. The work may consist of chores necessary for the daily housekeeping, such as catching fish and cultivating the vegetables that are to be eaten.

Then comes the morning session of teaching in *general subjects*. An earlier account (Hamre 1994a) gives as examples »Bengali and history of religion«. The teaching of the national language, which still in 1998 was a high priority, is primarily aimed at the fair number of students who are either illiterate or have had only a year or two of schooling. In 1994 there was a local Muslim clergyman, a mullah, who taught the history of religion. According to Hamre's account the mullah retold a passage from the Koran, which was then commented upon and applied to the contemporary world. In 1998 this subject was in the hands of the principal. Just as at morning assembly, when he read from both the Koran and the Bhagavad Gita, he based his teaching on a collection of texts from various religions. He himself described his teaching as »moral education«.

After a communal lunch, there was work on practical subjects, for which the students sign up according to their *individual* wishes. A report of 1987 (Final Evaluation Study) lists the following options:

- tailoring
- fish farming
- reed and bamboo work
- agricultural studies
- bee-keeping
- land surveying
- rope making
- electrical studies

A report of 1994 states that tailoring is the most popular subject among the women; fish farming is the men's favourite. In 1998 the lessons in cabinet-making and welding were well attended by young men. Among women, sewing was still at number one. The products of these small workshops may be used by the school itself, as for instance, chairs and tables made in the joinery workshop. Other products may be sold, thus providing a source of income for the school. This applies to articles like some agricultural products and skilfully welded gratings and metal gates made in the forge - but both in modest amounts.

We can try to put the activity of the school into perspective in two ways. We may try to shed further light on the school's background and basic ideas, and we may try to get an impression of the school's significance in the local community. The retrospective view came out in an interview done in March 1998 with the principal *Saif Uddin Ahmed*. Principal Ahmed told about his personal background: he was born and bred in the village in which the school is. His father, who was involved

*Saif Uddin Ahmed, principal of Khanjahania Gonobidyalaya. Photo by Gunhild Skovmand Jensen, 1999.*

in social work, inspired his son at an early age to get involved on behalf of society's very lowliest members.

In 1966, after passing his final examination at Bagerhat College, Mr Ahmed set up a school in his home village. The school, which now has over 600 pupils, included both primary and secondary schools. After taking part in the war of liberation in 1971, Mr Ahmed spent some years studying law. A crucial turning-point came in 1980, when he attended a countrywide conference held in Comilla on the topic »Rural Development«. A resolution was adopted to set up four gonobidyalayas in various parts of the country. Mr. Ahmed must, therefore, have participated in the epoch-making meeting at the school in Panchagram on 15.9.1980.

Then one thing led to another. Mr Ahmed's brother, who at that time was chairman of the »Union Council« roughly equivalent to a county council, supported the idea of setting up a gonobidyalaya in the area. In January 1981, Mr Ahmed was put in charge of the school project. Teaching began in 1982 in premises made available by the local authorities. After a site had been presented to the project and a grant from DANIDA had made it possible for them to erect their own buildings, activities could commence on the present site in 1986. Since then the staff has consisted fairly constantly of four full-time teachers, including the principal, of a couple of hourly-paid teachers and office and kitchen staff.

Two factors are crucial to the future prospect: 1) securing the financial base and 2) relations with the local community. Regarding finances, the principal and his colleagues envisage a gradual rise in farming income from some recently acquired areas. However, it is still hard to see how the school would become self-financing in that way. Some subventions from outside would seem necessary for some time to come.

As for 2), relations with the local community, there was initially widespread scepticism locally about the new institution. The reason why this mistrust has turned to trust is partly that most of the students, after completing a course at the gonobidyalaya, have either been able to obtain work or, in the women's case, have been able to earn money, e.g. by sewing. The favourable attitude is also due to the school's initiative in holding literacy courses for illiterate adults. Thus in 1998, a total of 10 courses were held, with 25 participants on each. The instructors on these Adult Literacy Courses (ALC) are former students of the school after they have completed a supplementary course aimed at acquiring the necessary qualifications. All this came out of the interview with Principal Saif Uddin Ahmed.

The notes mentioned refresh one's memory of the fascinating experience it was to sit in on the ALC teaching. For the women, the lessons are held in the afternoon, for the men in the evening. The daytime teaching

*An evening lesson in literacy. The teaching is taking place in a private home out in a village. Note than in this case women and men are being taught at the same time.*

is given amid considerable attention from the village children and adult passers-by. In the evenings, when the teaching is done in pitch darkness, the teacher may meet the men on a narrow veranda only sparsely lit up by a flickering hurricane lantern. The pupils, who include illiterate older and younger people, participate in the courses seriously and with involvement. One senses that for them it is not some kind of entertainment.

At some point the visitor from outside is often called upon to say a few words to the company. With a view to gaining some insight into what is going on, it has proved fruitful on such occasions to ask the participants (through an interpreter!) about their motives for joining these courses. The replies may be grouped into two, according to whether the students say that in their view literacy meets a purely practical need or a more »spiritual« one, although it is not possible to make a consistent division here.

*Practical motives*

Literacy will make it possible to:

- sign one's own name
- keep accounts
- avoid getting on the wrong bus
- avoid giving the children something wrong because one is unable to read the labels on medicine bottles.
- read posters
- read a doctor's sign and therefore be sure one has come to the right place
- read contracts and avoid getting cheated.

*Spiritual motives*

If one is literate, one will be able to:

- read newspapers
- read inscriptions on shrines
- read prayers in Bengali and not just learn them in Arabic
- read religious book in Bengali.

While the first motive given seems to be concerned with the ability to acquire general, maybe political, information, the last three are of a clearly religious nature. A few times some women expressed their motivation in beautiful symbolic language. Achieving literacy would in their view mean that

- their children would not have to live in darkness
- both they and their children would not be »blind within the eyes«.

Although the replies were given through a translation, one clearly sensed how Bengali »is a language capable of expressing the finest modulations of thought and feelings« (Ziring, p. 4).

Some of the initial opposition to the schools came from the mullahs. As we have already seen, the school is in an area where Islam has a very visible presence with many mosques. The mullahs seem to have feared that the school represented an attempt to Christianize the younger generation. This fear was not unfounded, as a number of the schools they knew about had been started by Christian missions.

As time has passed, the mullahs have become convinced that no such aim lies hidden behind the setting up of the school and all its activity. Probably local people have made it clear that, as we have seen in our list of motives above, literacy may have a positive religious value. Also, the school has from time to time invited one of the mullahs to teach (see above). Finally, some of the mullahs have turned up unannounced and, thus, discovered that the adult education did not contain any kind of religious propaganda. But crucial factors in this favourable development have been the principal's and his influential family's deep roots in the local context and their personal efforts for the people's benefit.

## Panchagram Gonobidyalaya

This school lies 70-80 km south-east of Dhaka near the large city of Comilla, which is an important traffic junction. Although the report of 1987 (Final Evaluation Study) shows that the school had a limited scope there are a number of later testimonies to favourable results as regards improving the conditions of the students. Also, the school is of historical interest, as it is, as we have already mentioned, the oldest of the five gonobidyalayas.

It was not possible to interview the principal, who was on a study trip to Denmark. Instead, an older dignified man named *Mosharraf Hossain* offered to tell about the origins and current problems of the school.

Mosharraf Hossain's interest in getting involved in the life of the school, as a member of the local governing bodies and in other ways, went back a long way. As a younger brother of the first principal, he had been able to watch the school's growth and work from the outset. The father of the brothers, who had occupied a prominent position in the local community, was mentioned as a co-founder of Panchagram Gonobidyalaya. Among the current urgent problems of the school he mentioned that some of the local supervisors were more interested in arranging things for their own benefit than in supporting the school's development for the benefit of the whole local community. In Mr Hossain's view, the way ahead was for the statutes of the General Council of the school to be amended so that the members were appointed by »selection instead of election«. Concerning the importance of the institution in the local context, Mr Hossain stated that the school had been of positive value in particular for young poor people, who otherwise easily went off the rails. Another positive effect was that literacy in the school's catchment area was considerably higher than in the adjacent areas.

At the school the interviewer was fortunate enough to meet a former student, a young woman called *Shapna*. Her story was another example of how Panchagram Gonobidyalaya had been important in motivating the young people of the locality. Shapna told us that after her time at the school she had obtained work in a clothing factory in Dhaka. Here she had a long working day, from 7 a.m to 10 p.m. The good wages, including overtime, had enabled her to obtain a small bank loan, which made it possible for her to give her family a rainproof roof over their heads. Her father, who was a barber and had no real property, had not been able to obtain the required amount. This perceptible financial advance was not to continue, however; Shapna was sacked when the factory was taken over by Koreans. The new owners decided that a knowledge of English was a requirement for continued employment.

Now the question was how Shapna was to advance. She herself most wanted to go to college for further education. But her family required her financial support right away. She considered taking out a loan through the students' union to enable her to buy a sewing-machine with a view to starting her own production of clothing. To what extent this idea will be feasible is unknown. But the example shows with all clarity that there is also an urgent need for new additional opportunities to be provided for those young people who have been given a step up the ladder by the school. For Shapna, for instance, it would be of considerable help to be given the chance of learning English at evening school at the same time as living and working at home.

## Central Gonobidyalaya

Central Gonobidyalaya differs from the four others in not being named after its location in a particular district or nearby town. It is named from its position, which is best described as »central«. Its geographical location is in the centre of the country, as close as possible to the capital, only some 20 km south-east of Dhaka. This school is not in any dominant position as regards the other gonobidyalayas. The overall control is still with BACE's office in Dhaka. But the school's position is central, because this institution is a centre for a number of activities carried out on behalf of all the schools. There is a profound symbolism in the fact that Central Gonobidyalaya is located on the edge of the town of Sonargaon. This »golden town« (the meaning of the name) was once, long ago in pre-Islamic days and up to the beginning of the seventeenth century, the country's capital. *Sonargaon* was thus the real centre of a number of important communal activities until the capital was moved to Dhaka.

A report of 1994 (Final Report. Midterm Review) shows that Central Gonobidyalaya, the newest of the five gonobidyalayas, was erected in 1994-95. It also shows that this new institution, besides functioning as an »ordinary« gonobidyalaya, was also meant to discharge several special functions, which the Report summarizes under three headings:

- to teach former students from the other gonobidyalayas
- to give further training to the teachers of the schools
- to carry on curricular development

In reports printed later, we find a number of additional points. They show that the duration of the *further training courses* for the students is set at four weeks, and that the aim is to give further training to 30 students at a time. With a view to strengthening interaction among the students and between teachers and students, these courses are residential courses, i.e. the students live at the school for the period of the courses. For this reason it has been found necessary for separate courses to be held for men and women. Regarding the content of the further courses, it is noted that the overall aim is leadership training aimed at equipping the students to play a leading role in the social development of their own local context. Therefore, the training includes teaching about how leadership qualities are developed, how an organization is run, and how decisions are arrived at democratically. The need to meet requirements for further vocational training, »additional skill training«, takes second place.

As for the second of the three points, the *further training of the teachers*, we find that now these courses are also being offered to the *administrative staff* of the schools. The widening of the target group means that this further training includes not only educational practice but also management development. Central Gonobidyalaya has yet another option available to the administrative staff, as the clerical employees are invited to special seminars along with the chairmen and members of the *local governing bodies*.

The third point, curricular development, is only briefly mentioned. Orally, we have been informed that this work is done in four kinds of collaboration, i.e.

- among the teachers at Central Gonobidyalaya
- between Central Gonobidyalaya and the staff of the other four schools
- between Central Gonobidyalaya and the BACE office in Dhaka
- between the teachers of the gonobidyalayas and educational consultants from Denmark.

*Dildur Mahmud, principal of Central Gonobidyalaya.*

Finally, these measures help to strengthen mutual contacts among all those who in some way are concerned with the gonobidyalaya project.

Regarding the future of the institution, Mr *Dildur Mahmud*, the principal of the school since 1996, tells us that the setting up of Central Gonobidyalaya has succeeded in giving the students more and more varied training opportunities. For instance, at a student course about to commence, women will be offered the chance of working on electrical installations. It will also be the aim in future to expand steadily the range of options for the young people.

Among wishes for the future are mentioned more short courses, which would however require increased teaching resources. Also mentioned is the desirability of setting up vocational guidance which could help the young students find work when their schooling was over. Also emphasized was the importance of the students' human development. On this point, as the section on the setting of objectives showed, the principal is very much in harmony with both Freire and Grundtvig.

## Uchai Gonobidyalaya

Uchai Gonobidyalaya is in the north-western corner of the country. As we have said, the school is one of the two oldest gonobidyalayas. According to the pamphlet by Mokammel & Gofur (p.4) it was set up back in the autumn of 1980, at almost the same date as Panchagram Gonobidyalaya. The pamphlet also mentions that a village doctor named Dr Rustam Ali, who worked in the area around Uchai, developed some ideas about adult education in the country districts. On the basis of conversations with Dr *Rustam Ali* (January 1999), who is also known as Dr Rustam Ali Mondal, more of the background history can be sketched in:

- Dr Rustam Ali, in collaboration with a professor from Bogra, started a »*Community University*« (apparently university extension college) in the area back in 1978.
- this was non-formal tuition held once a fortnight
- the subject was health, which is hardly surprising
- the teaching was done in the open air, under a Banyan tree.

In conclusion Dr Ali, who is a dignified seventy-year-old, told us that he was busy writing the history of the gonobidyalayas. All those interested should watch out for this project.

The school's timetable follows the general pattern of the gonobidyalayas: about 60% of teaching time is allocated to general subjects, and about 30% to vocational courses. The remaining 10% is spent in communal activities, particularly performing the practical work that is required (»Shramdan«). Available reports along with one pamphlet and an interview with the principal *Mr M.M. Rahman* all provide further details.

An early report of 1987 (Final Evaluation Study) comments that there are not very many courses being offered, in fact only four, but it also adds that Uchai breaks new ground in teaching midwifery. Another special feature noted in the report is that a woman teaches religious studies at this school.

»Introducing Uchai Gonobidyalaya« is a pamphlet of six columns. It is not dated, but must have been written in 1997/98, as the students' union is mentioned, see below. The pamphlet lists the courses offered under as many as 15 points. The first 11 courses are of a general character. They are:

1. Bengali, i.e. the teaching of the mother tongue. (We have been informed orally that the teaching is given in two groups, one for students with very little previous knowledge and one for the more

advanced).
2. Arithmetic
3. Social studies
4. History
5. Moral Education
6. Health & Nutrition.
7. Midwifery & Family Planning.
8. Agriculture (general).
9. Poultry
10. Pisciculture (i.e. fish farming)
11. General Knowledge (according to oral information this includes geographical knowledge).
12. Farm mechanics, including welding and motor-cycle repair.
13. Carpentry.
14. Electricity.
15. Sewing, including batik and dyeing.

As this shows, there is a rich assortment of courses on offer.

In addition the school carries on a number of educational activities directed towards the local population. One of the latest quarterly reports (BACE 1998) mentions three such outreach initiatives, including the literacy courses, known as ALC courses, which are also held by the other four gonobidyalayas.

However, the report gives some interesting details which clearly show the local people's involvement in the courses.

As at the other schools, 10 courses are held in Uchai, with around 25 adults on each, thus a total of 250. The report says that seven of the ten classes are made up of women, and three of men. Of the 250 enrolled students, 24 have subsequently dropped out, i.e. a drop-out rate of below 10%. The completion rate is of course also important. On five of the 10 classes, all the lessons have been held. On the others, the completion rate was between 94 and 98%.

The report also describes a quite extraordinary outreach that might be characterized as *religious education* for adults. This was a »Seminar-/Workshop« to which the local community was invited. Speakers at the seminar held on 28 December 1998 i.e. at the beginning of Ramadan, were two Muslim clerics. 71 attended, 52 men and 19 women. The topic was »The Role of Ramadan on Self-Rectification«, a subject of a moral and religious character. The content of the presentations is summed up in four points:

1. The word »Ramadan«, its linguistic and deeper meaning.
2. The importance of Ramadan for self-improvement - according to Hadith (the traditions about the prophet)
3. The importance of Ramadan for self-rectification - in the light of the Koran.
4. The unique significance of the practice of fasting in one's relations with Allah.

It is clear that this is religious instruction of a confessional nature. It is quite a different kind of religious and moral teaching from that we mentioned under the Khan Jahania Gonobidyalaya, which brought in other religions.

Finally, I should like to point out the sections in this report that deal with the »Ex-Students' Association« and its activity. This is described as »newly formed«. Conversations with board members show that this association was formed in 1997. The report also relates that the association has 311 members, and that it has at its disposal a fund of slightly more than 40,000 taka (£450-500). The money is used for giving small and rapid loans, »pump-priming« grants, for instance for fresh planting of agricultural areas. Normally the loans run for half a year. As of December 1998 a total of 85 such loans had been granted.

The advancing of small loans seems to make up an important part of the association's objects and activity. Among other activities, it is mentioned that the committee holds meetings three times a quarter and that a workshop of all members is called once a quarter. The last workshop held, on 16.12.98, gathered 118 people, 66 men and 52 women, roughly equally divided. In the brief summary of the discussion topics, difficulties in collecting membership dues are mentioned a couple of times. However, the repayment of loans is not mentioned as a problem.

The threads which connect the school with the local community are thus of many kinds. The network that has been created with the constantly growing Students' Association offers positive future opportunities.

## *Rangunia Gonobidyalaya*

In several respects Rangunia Gonobidyalaya differs from the other four. Geographically, the centre is somewhat on its own, in the lengthy »finger« that stretches down towards Burma. It is also located in a mountainous area, whereas the other schools are on the flat land between the rivers. Finally, the population is of more varied composition than is the case in the localities around the other four gonobidyalayas. Not only is the area home to about 15 different tribal peoples, a broad range of religions are also represented. Here we find not only adherents of Islam, Hinduism, and aboriginal tribal religions, but a considerable number profess Buddhism. This is perhaps scarcely surprising in view of the closeness to Burma.

The background history and first years of this gonobidyalaya have been related above. They ran into unforeseen difficulties relatively soon. One factor that seems to have sparked off disputes was that from the very beginning it was not quite clear who owned the site and the buildings. These frictions meant that the institution had to close for three years, from 1986 to 1989. As matters gradually clarified, it was possible to resume operations.

In its content, the teaching carried out at Rangunia was very close to the curriculum of the other gonobidyalayas. For instance, in the year 1994/95 they offered a number of vocational courses: the repair of electrical installations, cars, and agricultural machinery as well as welding and sewing. This is very similar to the programme quoted above for Uchai Gonobidyalaya. In addition, a later report of 1997 mentions teaching in Bengali, mathematics, history, and »moral education«. This is reminiscent of the programme at Khan Jahania Gonobidyalaya.

To ensure both the students' future opportunities and the survival of the institution, they have also gone in for agriculture. However, they have had to admit that the soil in this mountainous region is not suitable. There are far greater openings in forestry. In that connection, they have planted 20,000 trees for timber, which however will not be ready for felling for about 15 years.

The school's outreach activity is shaped by its being set in a region where tribals make up a large part of the local population. In the present year (1999/2000) two women from this group are working as teachers on adult literacy courses (ALCs), and one of the courses has deliberately been located in a tribal area. From time to time a wish has been expressed for a special gonobidyalaya for these people. However, one may assess the chances of meeting this wish, there is no doubt that it does indicate that the school has become a popular institution.

In Rangunia too an Ex-Students' Association has been set up which meets four times a year. But the region is poor and money in short supply. As far as is known, it has not yet been possible to grant the much sought-after short-term loans. But a beginning has been made. And the important thing is that the younger generation has become co-operation-minded. Here, the lines reach back to the Swarnivar movement and forward to a modern co-op movement.

# SOME RELATED INITIATIVES

In Bangladesh the teaching of adults does not take place only at the gonobidyalas. As we have mentioned, adult education is an element in several of the aid projects that have started up in Bangladesh. Examples are the twelve »Training and Resource Centres« that are run by the organization BRAC (see Smilie 1997). The interesting point for us in the present context, however, is not so much the way adult education is organized as whether this activity is conducted with a clear awareness of a link with the Danish folk-high-school tradition. In the following we shall first point to two examples of institutions that are independent of BACE but where such an awareness is nevertheless plainly present. Then we will present an institution which used to be linked with BACE but where awareness of Grundtvig and the folk high school cannot be documented.

## *Protiggya Parishad*

Protiggya Parishad is a small private organization whose work is based in a single modest complex of buildings located near the large town of Comilla in south-eastern Bangladesh. One of Protiggya Parishad's most extensive teaching projects, which is partly conducted out in the villages, is named the *Community School Project*. It was commenced in July 1995.

The educational activity of the organization in some respects resembles the gonobidyalaya projects, as is indicated, for instance, by the fact that a new pamphlet of January 1998 describes the centre as the gonobidyalaya of the district: Bejoypur Gonobidyalaya. The same pamphlet emphasizes that the institution is inspired by »Grundtvig's philosophy and style of teaching«. All the same, Protiggya Parishad does differ on some points from the gonobidyalayas we have mentioned. For instance, Protiggya Parishad is a somewhat more recent organization, which started up in 1988.

One essential difference is that unlike the five gonobidyalayas, Protiggya Parishad does not come under the umbrella of BACE, but right from 1996/97 has had its own independent collaboration with FFD and DANIDA. Even though Protiggya Parishad has its own overall management, its private status has not precluded it from receiving grants from public funds for a period.

*Fatema Kabir. Chair of governors of Protiggya Parishad.*

Finally, there is a difference in the way the tuition is organized. At the gonobidyalayas general education and practical work are combined in one single course lasting eight months. Protiggya Parishad operates with a basic course of six months, where »literacy training« is at the centre but is supplemented by elementary health and social studies. On the basis of this general education, it is reckoned that some of the students, probably some 30%, will be able to continue on special vocational courses. For the women, there are four-month courses in sewing and cooking. For the men, there are technical courses lasting up to a year or shorter agricultural courses of 2-4 weeks. The students completing further training should then be able to function as leaders and resource personnel in their local context.

However, there are strong lines of connection and conspicuous similarities between Protiggya Parishad and the gonobidyalaya projects.

Firstly, we must mention the *personal contacts*. The chairman of the board of Protiggya Parishad, *Mrs Fatema Kabir*, has for a period of 4 years, from 1985 to 1989, been the director of BACE. Furthermore, FFD has assisted Protiggya Parishad in various ways, e.g. with educational counselling. Finally, the director of Protiggya Parishad, *Mr Abdur Rahim*, for a number of years has been employed by the Noakhali project (see above) and in that connection has gained insight into Danish aid work and the Danish educational tradition.

Another similarity that should be mentioned is in the type of clientèle. Protiggya Parishad, like the gonobidyalayas, caters for the young people in the rural districts who are either completely illiterate or have had only a few years of schooling. These are the young people who have difficulty in obtaining and keeping paid work. However, a closer investigation of the clientèle reveals some differences. Whereas the age group for which the gonobidyalayas cater, consists of youngsters between 15 and 25, the framework is rather wider for Protiggya Parishad: 15-35. Furthermore, in enrolling students the gonobidyalayas aim at a rough balance between men and women, while Protiggya Parishad has a clear policy of giving women priority as they are felt to have greater problems than men. They reckon therefore that out of 2500 students, some 1500 (about 60%) will normally be women.

There is an important similarity in the *content of the teaching*, in that both organizations combine general and practical subjects. There may be a difference in structure and organization, but in this basic respect there is agreement. The reason for this is no doubt that this type of training is particularly needed in the rural areas of Bangladesh.

Both organizations stress the *further training of teachers*. Within Protiggya Parishad, this is done through courses of a fortnight or workshops lasting a couple of days. Among the gonobidyalayas the central institution is active in this area. In both organizations, leader training is built into these personnel courses.

Finally, both organizations stress that those students who have completed the courses on offer should also be given the *financial basis* for getting started in work. Opportunities can be created in several ways. Either these people, if they get a job, can be encouraged to make savings. Or they can be helped to obtain an establishment loan either by having a bank loan underwritten, or, as at Uchai, by the students' association administering a loan fund.

On the subject of the *daily teaching*, its challenges and opportunities, the school's teachers said that they faced two major challenges: teaching the totally illiterate, and teaching in a way that activated the students. The illiterate students had no foundations to build upon. As for activation, the students did indeed have plenty of motivation, but they cannot imagine that they themselves are expected to do anything beyond taking in and repeating what the teacher has said. That is what they know, or have heard, that teaching is. To alter this preconceived idea is enormously demanding.

In reply to the question how they set about the cultural component of the general education, the teachers replied that the options were many. For literature, Tagore obviously plays a very important part. But Muslim writers, both older and more recent ones, are also brought in. The form of teaching is particularly re-telling and reading aloud and discussion of selected short texts. It is unrealistic to expect the students to be able to work on texts they have read for themselves. As examples of activating forms of organization, they mentioned excursions to places of historical interest. These might be a Hindu temple or ruins of Buddhist buildings, known as »Buddhist relics«. Besides, dancing and singing were used, which, as at the gonobidyalayas, were particularly popular forms of activity.

Finally, in our conversation it came out that the frontier to the Indian state of Tripura was only a few kilometres to the east. One of the teachers, who had been born and bred in this frontier region, belonged to one of the tribal people. She stressed the value of including the tribal culture in the teaching. In her view, they could in this respect learn a lot from India, where tribal culture is the object of much greater interest than in Bangladesh.

As regards the *future of the project*, Fatema Kabir said in an interview (19.3.98) that the overall aim must of course be for everyone to learn to read and write. With this target in view, it would be desirable for each region to have responsibility for organizing its own project. In that connection it is important to aim for a change of attitude in the population. The greatest problem is that so many feel no concern. Far too many accept an »educational apartheid« as an immutable fact of nature (cf. Kabir 1995 p. 27).

Next, Fatema Kabir stresses that it is important to have firm regional roots that allow scope for local ethnic groups and other minorities in order to combat a nationalistic ideology, which would, she feels, be detrimental to the growth of world-wide community. These thoughts have been expounded by Fatema Kabir in an undated manuscript »A Philosophy for World Education«. The organizational structure of a local project does not need to be ponderous or costly. In Fatema Kabir's view it is not necessary, as in Denmark, to build large institutions where the students can live while they are taught (»residential education«). The education can and should be given in the villages themselves, in or just outside the houses where people live. That the essential thing is to make the best use of the resources that are actually available is expressed in a local saying: »Cut your clothes according to your cloth!«

## The MUL Center

MUL is an abbreviation of Mannobik Unnayon Lokkho. The English translation is »Human Resources Development«. Others have grasped the symbolic significance of the fact that »mul« in Bengali means »root« and that the education has something to do with being rooted. The institution's own publications emphasize that it is a »school for life«. The centre lies on the outskirts of the city of Nilphamari in the far northern end of Bangladesh. It is claimed that in clear weather it is possible to see the Himalayas, which are about 100 km due north.

The MUL Center is an educational institution run by the *Danish Santal Mission*. In Bangladesh this society is part of the Bangladesh Lutheran Mission which, as the name indicates, is an amalgamation of several Lutheran missions. In this case societies based in Denmark, Norway, and the USA are concerned. The *Santals* are an Indian tribal people. In the time before the immigration of the Aryans about 1500 B.C. they inhabited the area which later became the British province of Bengal and the Indian state of Assam. As several other ethnic groups, including the Indo-European Bengalis, gradually settled in these regions, the Santal areas are nowadays separated not only by several hundred kilometres, but also by the frontiers between India, Nepal, and Bangladesh.

The mission among the Santals was started in 1867 by the Dane H.P. Børresen (1825-1901) and the Norwegian Lars Skrefsrud (1840-1910). Still today the locality in which the mission began, which lies northwest of Calcutta (NB near Tagore's Shantiniketan) is inhabited by Santals. Right from early days Grundtvigian groups were among the backers of the Santal Mission. While on a visit to Denmark, H.P. Børresen forged this link, which has existed ever since.

In the independent state of Bangladesh, the Danish Santal Mission started a hospital work among leprosy patients in 1976. Twenty years later, in 1996, the work and the premises were taken over by the International Leprosy Mission. The mission's educational activities are directed towards both children and adults; it not only runs 37 village schools, but also offers several forms of adult courses. Among these we can mention basic courses in English and computer technology. The initiative also includes a »folk high school project«, which commenced in 1995. The main features of this activity will now be outlined.

A brochure called »About MUL-Center«, summarizes the institution's distinctive features in four points: The centre is (a) a folk high school, (b) a residential training facility at which young people of both sexes are taught at the same time, (c) a place where knowledge is acquired and where a mutual interplay and exchange of ideas takes place, and (d) an institution which gives the students skills that will make it easier for them to obtain work. Apart from the residential nature of the centre, these points could also apply to the gonobidyalayas. The following information, shows, however, that there are considerable differences.

First, we note that although the age range of 15-25 is the same, enrolment at the MUL Centre requires a minimum qualification of a school-leaving examination from secondary school, i.e. 10 years of schooling. The gonobidyalayas and Protiggya Parishad were open to illiterates and to young people with only a few years schooling. Another big difference is in payment. At the gonobidyalayas the students are given not only free tuition, but also a modest daily allowance to make up for the loss of the family income. At the MUL Center the students pay 500 taka (about £6 or $9) for tuition and 50 taka as an enrolment fee.

The classes at the MUL Center are not so large: 10 women and 10 men, as against the 30 + 30 at the gonobidyalayas. And the teaching is organized in a different way, as the MUL Center operates with two sessions annually each of five months.

The content of the teaching given at the centre is divided into three sections. First, a »Basic Course« is held, the subjects being the culture, language, and history of the country. Then follows a main vocational course, with a fixed rotation between (1) Teacher training aimed at teaching in Primary School, (2) Social development work, or (3) Health studies. In addition, the students can sign up for special courses like leadership training, home economics, management, computer technology, and English.

The last phase of the process focuses on practical work. This may involve what are known as mini-projects which are carried out at the centre, e.g. looking after domestic animals, fish-farming, and market gardening. There is also two weeks' fieldwork at an external institution that works in the relevant field, i.e. within education, social work, or the health sector.

No specifically religious instruction is given at the centre. However, the brochure stresses that the school emphasizes »moral and spiritual life«. An ethical training is, however, integrated both directly and indirectly into the life of the school. As at the gonobidyalayas, each morning commences with the students lining up by the flagstaff in quiet and orderly straight lines. After some simple gymnastic exercises to sha-

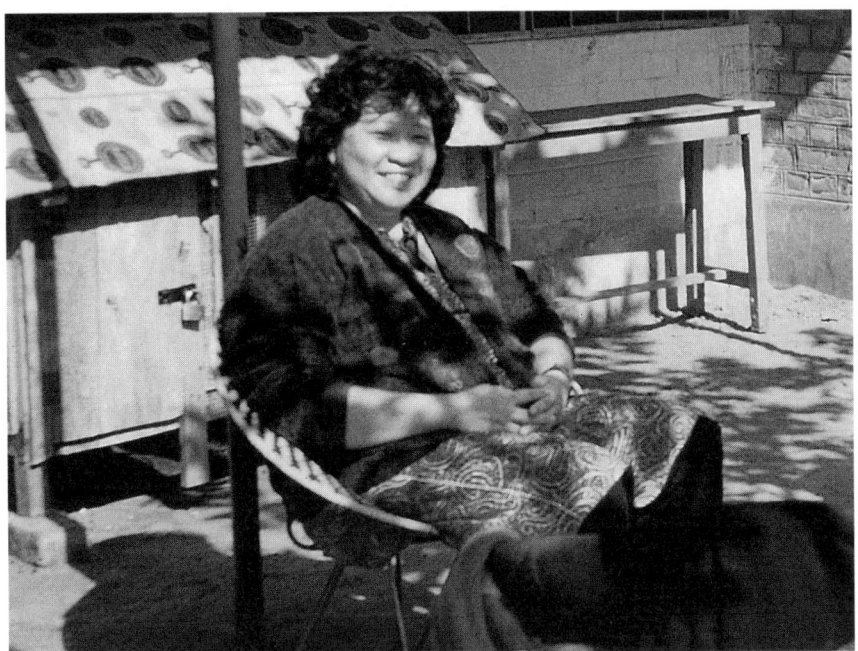

*Teresa Chai, administrative head of MUL Center, Nilphamari.*

ke off the remnants of the morning cold, the flag is raised and the national anthem sung. This helps to foster an awareness of national identity and a community spirit that transcends social and religious barriers. Ethical training is given more indirectly in the way that it is taken for granted that the school's rules of behaviour will be kept.

As regards the students' *spiritual* development, reference is made to the importance of the individual subjects and to the consideration that is paid to the religious adherence of the students. Since the students include Muslims, Hindus and Christians, the timetable does allow for the festivals and holy days of these religions to be celebrated according to custom.

The responsibility for planning and carrying out the teaching is in the hands of the principal, Mrs *Joanna Suprobha Howlader*, who was born and bred in the country. The administrative leader or »Superintendent« is Rev. *Teresa Chai*, who comes from Malaysia. She took her basic theological training in her homeland and then took further education in the USA. She became acquainted with Grundtvig's educational ideas during two visits to Denmark, where she combined studies at Copenhagen University with stays at two folk high schools.

In a conversation about the centre's future, Teresa Chai first focused on the *Business Training Centre*, which was set up in 1997 in the city of

Rajshahi as a division of the MUL Center. As the name suggests, this catered primarily for the acquiring of skills relevant to office work, such as computer technology and English. General subjects like culture, language, and history were not neglected, however. Now, as of spring 1999, this centre seems about to be wound up. Although there were sufficient applications, the outcome of the teaching did not measure up to expectations. It has been shown that the general knowledge of the students was too limited for them to be able to get beyond a quite elementary mastery of language and technology.

The MUL Center has, after a brief probationary period in 1995, been functioning for three whole years. Experience has been positive. Having both women and men in residence has caused no problems. Also, it has been shown that on the whole former students have found work. The combination of academic and practical subjects has apparently meant that the students have been employable, or, as Teresa Chai puts it, »marketable«.

## Santosh

In drawing this section to a close, we must emphasize a gonobidyalaya-like project that is easily overlooked because it is not mentioned in the printed descriptions of these schools, but only in unprinted background documents. This silence is probably due to the fact that this project was abandoned fairly early on. Apart from the usefulness of sometimes also studying abandoned projects, the Santosh initiative is interesting for its particular history. In one of Uffe Geertsen's articles he mentions that at various places in Bangladesh educational activities have been started on a local level, among them:

> »initiatives taken mainly by Islamic organizations. A little was going on before, somewhat more is now under way: Handicraft courses for the girls, agricultural courses for the young men... (Højskolebladet 1983, p. 631).«

We here note the plural »initiatives«. Thus there were several. However, only one of them collaborated for some years with the gonobidyalaya projects co-ordinated by BACE.

The educational centre of Santosh is located outside Tangail about 130 km north-west of Dhaka. It was set up in 1968 by the prominent politician and educational reformer *Maulana Abdul Hamid Khan Bhashani* (1885-1976). »Maulana« is a Muslim honorific that means »Master«, rather similar to the Hebrew »Rabbi«.

It is told of Bhashani's life and work that in the period before Indian independence he was the leader of the Muslim League in Assam, one of the north-eastern provinces. After 1947 he moved back to his home area in the Tangail district. Bhashani combined his basic Islamic view with strong left-wing political views. He spoke up for the small farmers and agricultural workers against the wealthy landowners; in foreign policy he advocated that Pakistan should link itself with China. Disappointed at the gradual rapprochement with the USA, he abandoned politics.

Bhashani's efforts towards educational reform aimed at creating a special school system with a view to assisting the advance of the poor rural population. The new schools he envisaged were characterized by three qualities: (1) They were to be organized in a coherent system in which all types of schools, from nurseries to universities, would form an integrated whole. (2) The education was to give top priority to practical skills needed by the rural population. (3) The new system was to be based on Islam's universal common human values:

- respect for manual work
- equality among human beings
- the duty to serve one's fellow human beings

Bhashani's Islamic humanism is again an expression of the particular Bengali version of Islam we have already noted.

The adult education centre in Santosh builds upon these ideas. In 1981 when the institution joined in BACE's application for aid from Denmark, the centre's activities included the following:

(a) an agricultural college named Islamic University Technical College
(b) two secondary schools, one for boys and one for girls
(c) a home for orphans (in 1981: 300).

The plans for the future for which aid was sought included, besides a literacy programme, the setting-up of facilities for practical instruction, including a printing-press, a workshop, a weaving workshop, along with the teaching of agriculture and the care of fish-farms.

The collaboration with BACE seems to have ceased some time in 1984-85. The reasons can only be guessed. We might think of the escalation of the Islamization process that took place in the 1980s. The institution may then have received the necessary support from public grants.

The Santosh centre is akin to the gonobidyalaya projects primarily in the clientèle for which it caters: the poorest part of the rural population.

There is also broad agreement on the practical, vocational aim of the teaching. But there are undeniable differences too.

Organizationally, the obvious difference lies in Bhashani's vision of a large unified school system embracing all levels from nursery to university. The sparse documentation that exists gives no hint of any knowledge of Grundtvig and the folk high school. To this we must comment that the connection between the Santosh centre and the gonobidyalayas co-ordinated by BACE was broken off at least two years before BACE's collaboration with FFD was formalized, and a direct connection with the Danish folk high schools came about. None the less, it is interesting to consider whether a partnership could have worked under such new conditions. If the Santosh centre, despite the fundamentalist currents of the time, could have held on to the founder's open humanist views, a collaboration might not have been impossible. In any case, it would have broadened the minds of both parties.

# LINKS WITH GRUNDTVIG

*Folk high schools and Gonobidyalayas*

*Context and further development*

The people and organizations behind the setting-up of the gonobidyalaya project in the years around 1980 considered it worthwhile to test out whether the Danish folk-high-school idea might help to promote favourable community development in Bangladesh. So how has this experiment turned out?

In the years that have passed, repeated evaluations have been made in an attempt to compile an audit of the negative and positive outcomes of the initiative. The first question that has been asked in this context is whether the high-school idea is capable of being realized at all in this unfamiliar setting. On the whole the answer has been positive. Although some part-initiatives have not worked as intended, it would seem proven that the gonobidyalayas have had a favourable, initiating effect - not just for the students, but also in the local community.

A second question, which has exercised particularly the Danish participants in the project, touches upon the relationship of the gonobidyalayas to the very idea of the folk high school. In other words, the question is asked whether we are justified in seeing the gonobidyalayas as a new kind of folk high school. Are they, or are they not? A thorough treatment of this question is to be found in the Final Report, Midterm Review, of December 1994, in which a whole section (7.4.3) discusses »the affinity« between the two forms of school.

This report starts by affirming that the affinity »is apparent«, but that there are differences both regarding the content of the tuition and regarding the students' motives in applying for acceptance at the schools. The major differences are summed up in four points:

### 1. The social background of the target groups

The Danish folk high schools appeal to a fairly well-educated and well-to-do segment of the population. The introduction to this section (p.50) refers to »a fairly well-educated and affluent peasantry«, which under Point 1 on p. 51 has been abbreviated to »a relatively well-educated part of the population.« The gonobidyalayas, in contrast, cater for the very poorest people and the uneducated part of the rural population. Many of the students are illiterate.

## 2. The age of the students

The students at the Danish folk high schools come from all age groups, from 17 upward, whereas the clientèle of the gonobidyalayas is recruited entirely from the age group 16-25.

## 3. The objectives of the institutions

The folk high schools offer non-formal leisure-time tuition beyond primary school level, whereas the gonobidyalayas offer primary education and elementary vocational training.

## 4. Residential or non-residential.

At the Danish folk high schools the students live at the school (»residential education«) and usually the teachers also live on the campus. This means that students and teachers spend a great deal of time together. The »special social atmosphere« that is created through hours spent together during leisure time and evenings, through discussion in small groups and in the spontaneous activities (games, dancing, sport, drama etc.) are regarded at the folk high schools as a sine qua non for speaking of a high school stay. None of these features are yet possible at the gonobidyalayas.

Nevertheless it will still be in order to point to an affinity between the gonobidyalayas and the Danish folk high schools. The common areas are to be found both in the content and also to some extent in »the didactic approach«.

## 1. Content

In both types of school, cultural activities (sport, games, singing) play an important role. This is also true of practical work (in Bangladesh called »shramadam«) which is planned and carried out by the students in partnership. All this fosters the development of »mutual understanding and responsiveness, team spirit and group consensus«.

## 2. Pedagogical approach

Both school types focus on the student's personal development, and this is a consequence of a student-centred and student-activating approach to teaching. In both contexts, the student's personal development is supported by fostering self-awareness and self-confidence through active participation in planning and performing the daily work; also through encouraging the expression of the student's own opinion and participation in free discussion and through group work and a project-centred didactic approach.

This detailed and judicious summing-up is a valuable aid to understanding the relation between the two forms of school. Both earlier and later writers have expressed themselves similarly, but not so extensively (e.g. Hamre 1994 a+b, Geertsen 1983, Skovmand Jensen 1989). It is also clear that the writers of this report have endeavoured to formulate their views in up-to-date terms.

Earlier in the 1994 Report (actually in Chap. 1) we are informed that the inspiration from the Danish folk high schools can be summarized under two points:

(a) »a student-centred and participatory approach«
(b) »emphasis on cultural awareness«.

One might say that Point 2 (pedagogical approach) makes specific and thus clarifies what is here summarized in Point a. On the other hand, Point 1 (Content) seems to have supplied an abbreviated version of all that, in the practice of the gonobidyalayas, is covered by the phrase »emphasis on cultural awareness«. In order to forge such an »awareness«, intensive work is done on language, literature, history, and social conditions. In all circumstances cultural awareness is an important concept. It is not only in the organizational forms referred to, but also in the work on the content of the cultural subjects, that the teaching helps to develop self-awareness and self-confidence.

What conclusion should we draw from such observations: that the gonobidyalayas are both like and unlike the Danish folk high schools? Firstly, it must be affirmed that this was precisely what was bound to happen as soon as any attempt was made to realize the high-school idea in the framework of a fresh national context. It is of the essence of the folk high schools that their activity should proceed in an ongoing dialogue with their own cultural and societal setting.

Secondly, it must be affirmed that it has at no time been the intention of the initiators and participants that the Danish folk high school should be carried over unchanged to Bangladesh. On the contrary. Adaptation was and is necessary. Back in Daniel Pedersen's presentation in 1977 that started it off, it was emphasized that although the preconditions were to some degree comparable, it was not the Danish folk high school as such that might prove useful in Bangladesh, but »something along those lines«.

Others since have expressed themselves similarly. Uffe Geertsen stressed in 1983 that the task was »to support and further develop« the educational initiatives that were already proceeding. In Bjørn Hamre's view, the contribution of the folk high schools might be to give a new inspiration (Hamre, 1994b). In the pamphlet by Mokammel and Gofur (1994/95), the authors are at pains to point out how an educational effort to benefit those groups in the weakest position in society has a long tradition in Bengali history. The statement of aims of 1994 that has been quoted states diplomatically that the gonobidyalayas are »based on« the idea of the folk high school (p.22). With this concentrated phrase they have managed to weld together two assessments: that there is both a link and a further development of the Danish concept.

## Discovering the Originator

Initially, it was the idea of the folk high school that caught on in Bangladesh. As time passed, Grundtvig was discovered, the father of the idea, and people were fascinated by his thinking. There is evidence that the transition from one stage to the next took place in the years after 1988, i.e. in the period after the BACE people and their staff had made contact with the Association for Folk High Schools in Denmark, actually with this association's international committee. In the years after 1988 the consultants of this committee paid several visits to Bangladesh and in conversations and on courses expounded the ideological basis of the folk high schools and, thus, also the ideas of Grundtvig. In addition, key persons in BACE and a number of other contact persons were invited to spend time in studying in Denmark. Here they gained personal knowledge of the folk high schools and they heard constantly about Grundtvig, the man with the strange concatenation of consonants in his name (»ndtv«).

How did they react to Grundtvig and his ideas? To put it another way: What happens to Grundtvig's pedagogical ideas as soon as they are slotted into a development situation, i.e. a setting shaped by the particular circumstances of the Third World in general and Bangladesh in particular? Firstly, something foreseeable happens: a selection and adaptation process takes place. Out of the copious arsenal of Grundtvig's ideas, people select those which seem especially relevant to the development situation, i.e. his educational ideas. And from among these, they select Grundtvig's thinking about a new kind of school for adults. They leave on one side, for the time being, his ideas about a reform of child education, of church schooling, or of university tuition. They then adapt Grundtvig's ideas to the existing opportunities. They have to, so that the ideas can work in practice.

But a third change takes place too: There is development in the interpretation of Grundtvig; new perspectives are discovered in what Grundtvig wrote and said. This sort of development is normally sparked off by one or more of the following factors:

- previously unknown texts come to light
- familiar thoughts and texts are placed in a fresh historical context or in a new current one
- ideas that arose in quite different contexts are used as »searchlights« on the material
- outward circumstances call for fresh priorities, i.e. a new conception of what is important and what is not.

In the case in view, the realizing of Grundtvig's educational ideas in Bangladesh, it is not very probable, indeed hardly possible, that hitherto unknown texts by Grundtvig will be found. The scattered printed comments and the interviews that have been held show that the following contexts and ideas of Grundtvig have made a particular impression, and these have therefore been appropriated and adapted so that fresh priorities have emerged:

1. The parallel between mid-nineteenth-century Denmark and present-day Bangladesh.
2. Education of the people.
3. The school for life.
4. Living interaction.
5. Freedom.
6. Setting fresh priorities.

## Development in the interpretation of Grundtvig

### 1) A historical view

In 1977, when Daniel Pedersen told about the 19th century background to the emergence of the folk high schools, the BACE people were »very interested« in hearing »about Denmark's situation at that time, which in exceedingly many areas was similar to that of Bangladesh today« (Hamre, 1994b). It was not the first time a similarity had been pointed out. It probably occurs first in Erica Simon's dissertation of 1960, the last chapter of which says that on many points a striking parallel (»un parallélisme frappant«) can be observed between nineteenth-century Denmark and the present-day Third World (Simon, 1960, p.715).

This similarity or parallel can be defined in different ways. For Daniel Pedersen it was important that »the people were illiterate, they were dying of cholera and tuberculosis, and Denmark was bankrupt after the Napoleonic wars« (Hamre ib). For Erica Simon the similarity was primarily that in both contexts people were in the midst of a cultural struggle, in the clash between an alien, imposed culture, and a homegrown, »folk« culture.

From subsequent years we can pick out three contributions to the debate. In a commentary upon Simon's views, Holger Bernt Hansen stresses the important difference that arises from the post-colonial situation of the third-world countries:

> »Striking parallels with other areas may be useful and instructive, but they may also blur the reality. The post-colonial situation itself raises problems and marks out front lines that are quite different from anything Scandinavia has experienced. In that way, the very process of creating a popular culture becomes quite different. (Hansen, 1968, p.14).«

Some twenty years later, a younger scholar, Stephen Borish, says that even though similarities are demonstrable regarding the rural population's poverty and the landowners' dominant role, there are a number of differences between the two situations. The most important would seem to be the great rural reforms, the abolition of serfdom in 1788 etc. (Borish, pp.414-418). The effect of these reforms was a crucial factor in the rise of the peasantry in the nineteenth century and, therefore, in the success of the folk high schools. The Danish context was discussed at a conference on the topic »Education and Development« held at Dhaka University in January 1999. One of the participants remarked that, in contrast to Denmark in the 1700s and 1800s, Bangladesh did not have sufficiently many influential and well-intentioned land-owners. To put it briefly, they lack enlightened absolutism. Finally, we shall quote the comment of Uffe Geertsen in one of his articles on the expectation that the gonobidyalayas might become »a kind of Bengali folk high schools.« Such a hope is audacious

> when one thinks of the enormous differences in background and situation between Denmark in 1844 and Bangladesh in 1983... There are resemblances too, but more in needs than in background. (Geertsen, p. 583).

'More in needs than in background'. This precise formulation may fittingly stand as a summary of the discussion. But however the »similarity« is assessed, it cannot be denied that it was in fact this historical view that at an early stage aroused interest in Bangladesh and was important as an inspiration. During the app. 15 years that have passed between the mid-eighties and the present time, principals, teachers and administrators involved in the gonobidyalaya-project have made acquanintance with Grundtvigian ideas about »popular enlightenment«, a »school for life«, and »living interaction«. Naturally, these ideas are understood on the basis of people's own background, and their content is prioritized on the basis of the current needs of present-day Bangladesh.

## 2) Popular enlightenment

The Danish word is »folkeoplysning«, which describes both an educational activity directed towards the people, the »folk«, and teaching whose content and method is »popular«, of the »folk«. In both cases, if we are going to understand the concept better, we are required to give some account of how the word »folk« (or »people«) is to be understood.

If we wish to discuss with those involved in the gonobidyalaya project the way the concept »folkeoplysning« (popular enlightenment) is to be understood, the term will usually have to be translated into English as »education of the people«. This has already begged the question of where the emphasis is to lie and we have come down in favour of the first option: the concept means education directed towards the people. This seems to be the dominant view. If we then ask who the »people« are in Bangladesh, the answer is always: »They are the poor backward part of the rural population«. The reports refer to this group as »the downtrodden people in a poor country« (Final Evaluation, 1987, Preface) or »the poor rural youth«. These people are backward in three respects:

(a) Socially and politically they are oppressed, »downtrodden«.
(b) Economically they are poor.
(c) Culturally they are backward. They are illiterate and they have »many primitive ideas and beliefs« as the Final Report (1996) puts it.

Mokammel and Gofur's pamphlet of 1994/95 characterizes the »people« for whom the gonobidyalayas cater with similar expressions:

(a) »downtrodden« (twice), »subaltern«, and »marginal groups.«
(b) »poor« (several times).
(c) »illiterate«, »school dropouts«.

With only a few variations, the description given in the reports is repeated here. According to these assessments, it is the task of »education for the people« to contribute to an »uplift« of that quite considerable part of the population which in three important respects lacks something that the privileged minority has. The next interesting point is the way the pamphlet describes Grundtvig and his educational ideas. Here the clientèle for which the Danish folk high schools cater is described with the expressions »the common man« (twice) and »the common masses« (pp 5-7). These translations of the Danish »folk« as it forms part of Grundtvig's thinking on »folk enlightenment« call for comment.

The last phrase (the masses) was well-known in Grundtvig's day, often the Danish word »Mængden« (the crowd) was used. About this Grundtvig said that the »People« (folk/nation) comprised more than what was described as the crowd or the masses. In one of his best-known high-school songs, Grundtvig stresses that »folk« and fatherland are more than the masses, the soil, and the beach. The people includes more than just the masses and the fatherland is more than just the givens of nature. The people comprises for Grundtvig not just the oppressed, poverty-stricken masses, but the whole population that has a shared language, a shared history, and shared values. The first phrase, the common man, is one Grundtvig would much prefer to the masses, if need be. In his writings of the 1840s, he discusses these concepts and defines their meaning:

> The common man is the kernel of the people, that part of the nation which literally eats its bread in the sweat of its brow... (It is stressed)

that the future actually belongs to the peasants, the craftsmen, with a good old-fashioned word the common man and with a new bad word, the masses, that is something I have both seen and said for a whole generation, and that is something that I have constantly exhorted both high and low to prepare themselves for...only a little earlier or later it must be the common man who has the decisive word in civic society (Bugge, 1965, p. 321-322).

For Grundtvig the »common people« are a section of the population, a part of the »folk«. But they are also more, they are the »kernel of the folk«. It is the common people who bear within them the positive qualities from which the future grows. In this kernel is found the positive »folkish« potential, which in the future can and should characterize the whole population. It is a similar assessment that leads him to describe the commonalty as »the common treasure« (GSkV II, 241).

Neither the reports nor the two authors discuss the adjective »folkelig« (popular, folkish, of the people). »Of the people« may imply both »for the people« and »from the people«. The word is exceedingly hard to translate (see Simon, 1960, p.59, note 22; Eichberg, 1992, Introduction). But attempts are occasionally made. At a conference held in Copenhagen in 1995, Keith Jackson, an Englishman, suggested »popular education« (Education...Progress, pp.9-9), with the explanation: »popular not in the sense that it is well supported but that it is of the people. It could be described as education for, and in response to, people as citizens.« A Dane might have misgivings. In Danish, »popular« has associations with what most people prefer, not what everyone needs in their capacity as citizens. But in the particular way the gonobidyalayas administer Grundtvig's ideas about »a school for life«, they have to a remarkable degree actualized the very kind of education Keith Jackson pointed to. An »education for, and in response to, people as citizens.«

## *(3) The school for life*

Whereas the concepts »folk« and »folkelig« were not so easy to deal with, it has been much easier to translate and explain the phrase »the school for life«. We would refer readers to a more detailed account, but we can set down here that the phrase »school for life« in Grundtvig's works describes education that

> (a) arises from life, i.e. it is rooted in the life of the individual and the people. It speaks into the life situation of the young, and it is inspired by the people's myths and history.

(b) is living. That is to say that the work of education is not based on the book, but on the living, spoken word, above all conversation (see below). A precondition for this being possible is that the mother tongue is the medium employed.
(c) aims at life. The education has the task of shedding light both on human life as such and on the individual's life. (Bugge, 1993, pp.20-22).

*On (a)*: The gonobidyalayas strive energetically and sincerely to make the teaching relevant to the life that the individual has to lead, including enabling the youngster who leaves the school to sustain a living by earning some money for him/herself. And the general part of the teaching regularly includes the history, cultural monuments, and current social issues of the country.

*On (b)*: In harmony with Grundtvig's thinking, oral instruction has always been the hallmark of folk high schools right from the beginnings in the mid nineteenth century. In this respect, too, the teaching at the gonobidyalayas is very much in accord with Grundtvig's educational ideas. For instance, the teaching of literature and history is only to a limited extent based on the students working with books. Initially, this is not due to considerations of principle, but practical factors. Many of the students are illiterate, for one thing, and first have to spend time learning to read and write. Books are also expensive to obtain.

As regards the use of the mother tongue in the teaching, Mokammel & Gofur tells us that this stipulation of Grundtvig's was really one that people in Bangladesh could relate to:

> This was a view we Bengalees immediately understand, as we are a rare nation in history, who has shed blood to maintain the sanctity of our language (p. 6).

The bloody struggle referred to, which was a struggle to retain the mother tongue, Bengali, has been briefly recounted on p. 15.

Among other traits which, in Grundtvig's educational universe help to make the teaching living, singing is important. At the gonobidyalayas this practice has been taken over. They sing happily and readily when they are together for communal lessons. And of the tuition at the MUL Center, we were told that they

> to a great extent build upon the Danish folk-high-school traditions with lessons in culture, language, history, and lots of singing. (Chai p. 9).

The local singing tradition is largely based on a single man or woman standing at the front and playing and/or singing to the others. Community singing, as we know it, is gaining ground, however. The young people love it. And as we have mentioned, at the Khan Jahania Gonobidyalaya they have recognized this and had a small local songbook printed. This means that the way has been opened for community singing to spread into the villages to which the students return home.

*On (c)*: Another important way in which the gonobidyalayas resemble the Danish folk high schools is that they are not examination schools. Their aim is not to enable the students to pass a particular exam. Their immediate aim is to enable the student to perform practical work whereby they can gain a living - and perhaps later, on the basis of loans or savings, start their own business. This vocational aim makes the gonobidyalayas differ from Danish folk high schools.

An important similarity between the two forms of schools is found in the long-term aim called education for life. Both the folk high schools and the gonobidyalayas aim to use their teaching to help the young people's understanding of human life. Of the teaching on offer at the gonobidyalayas, it is only within the very limited moral education that the concerns of human life are directly touched upon. However, the students can acquire an understanding of life indirectly, e.g. through the lessons in literature, history, and social studies.

One particularly important form of indirect education in understanding life is the joy in living that is created in a school with no exams. This joy gives rise to a fruitful wonder at life's possibilities. And the presence of joy in living is the very feature that several visitors have observed at the gonobidyalayas.

## *(4) Living interaction*

As is well known, Grundtvig considered it important that the teaching at the new schools he envisaged should be based on »the living Word«, and in his view this meant it should be based on dialogue between teacher and students and among the students. It is above all this »living interaction« that counts.

This idea of the crucial importance of conversation in an educational context was something quite new in Bangladesh in the early 1980s. An unprinted report by Ploug Olsen and Schultz Jørgensen (1982) shows that within the Noakhali project one-way communication was the only method used, i.e. the teacher lectured or gave instructions. The students were passive listeners.

*Cover of Tanvir Mokammel's book. The English translation of the title is: »Grundtvig and People's Education«.*

Initially, even principals and teachers at the gonobidyalayas had reservations about this new dialogue method. Within a few years it had been grasped, and as they have said themselves, the teachers discovered with surprise that the method worked amazingly well. In several contexts it is stressed that conversation has now become an essential part of the tuition given at the gonobidyalayas.

The principal of the Central Gonobidyalaya applied the term »participatory teaching« to the use of dialogue. And Mokammel & Gofur's pamphlet says that »the method of teaching is of participatory approach« (p.13). The student activation in view here is probably the feature that is referred to in the pamphlet about Protiggya Parishad, which says that the institution is »inspired by Grundtvig's philosophy and style of teaching.«

An especially intensive form of living interaction takes place at the gonobidyalayas' ALC courses, the adult literacy courses held in the afternoon or evening in private homes in the villages. Here it is possible to witness tuition that takes place in quite a narrow group of people, in which conversation flows about the great and marvellous opportunity: discovering a new world.

## (5) Freedom

In regard to the concepts »education of the people«, »the school for life«, and »living interaction«, the interpretation of Grundtvig in Bangladesh has predominantly focused upon the concrete, practical aspects of the teaching. When we come to the concept of »freedom«, the reverse is true. Here, interest has primarily been turned upon the theoretical principles concerning the whys and wherefores of the teaching. In that context the concept of »freedom« plays an important part. This is not by chance. It is largely because Paulo Freire names »liberation« as the highest goal of education.

In the latest statement of aims which was set out and commented upon above, Grundtvig's ideas were interpreted according to Paulo Freire's educational thinking. This is not a new approach. It is found in other third-world countries, too. An example close at hand in India can be cited: Asoke Bhattacharya's book »Empowering the Neoliterates« (Calcutta, 1994). It is not surprising that Grundtvig is understood on the basis of Freire. Freire has been known for decades, whereas Grundtvig is a relatively new acquaintance.

Against this background, it is important to be aware of a number of other concepts which, in Freire, are grouped around the concept of freedom and therefore impinge on the interpretation of Grundtvig. On this point, the question arises: to what extent do these accompanying concepts make suitable gateways to an understanding of Grundtvig's use of the word »freedom«? In what follows, we shall seek to answer the question in a fairly brief, provisional investigation, in which the interpretative model is applied to some relevant texts of Grundtvig.

In introduction, it will be useful to distinguish between negative and positive aims, i.e. the things one wishes to combat, and the things one wishes to promote. In Freire's terms, it is the NEGATIVE AIM of education to counter the duress and oppression that leads to the lower strata of society being inactive, exploited, and despised in the three areas mentioned above: the social-political, the economic, and the cultural. Briefly, they have been deprived of their humanity, they have been dehumanized.

The POSITIVE AIM is expressed using the terms that above (p.30) were characterized as accompanying concepts of »freedom«, i.e.

- *empowerment*, i.e. that the lowest population groups are given a lift-up socially and economically, and that, politically, they are equipped to exercise their democratic rights and thus, by their own active efforts, to improve their lot.
- *conscientization*, i.e. that the oppressed become conscious of their possibilities, abilities, and rights.
- *emancipation*, i.e. the achievement of freedom to think and speak, including in particular the freedom to use the mother tongue. On this, Freire in one of his works has described the literacy process, i.e. the work of learning to read and write, as a cultural action for freedom.
- *humanizing*, or re-humanizing, i.e. that the hitherto oppressed and silent strata of society find their voice, so that they too can achieve lives of human dignity.

To shed light on Grundtvig's thinking about the same subjects, we shall point to statements and views in his educational and political writings. Of the latter texts, particular interest attaches to the third volume of his periodical »Danskeren« (The Dane), of 1850. This volume (abbreviated to D III) appeared the year after the Danish Constitution was adopted in 1849. The anniversary of the Constitution in 1850 gave Grundtvig the opportunity for some reflections upon the »people's gain« from the introduction of democracy.

## Empowerment

As we might expect, Grundtvig expresses himself somewhat differently from Freire. In passionately rejecting that the Danish people should be »subjugated by Latin and ravaged by Germany« (GSkV II, 38), he is opposing cultural disempowerment. Grundtvig can express his NEGATIVE aim in a broader perspective and proclaim that he will do battle with »apathy, slave-mindedness... and all national and human wretchedness« (GSkV II, 229). Finally, the negative aim can also be expressed in a depth perspective arising from the contrast between life and death in Grundtvig's world of ideas. On this basis, the negative aim can be expressed with a word like »People-death«, i.e. the dissolution, destruction, or perishing of the people. The POSITIVE goal is of course the opposite: »Renewal of the People's Life« with a view to achieving the »the common best and general well-being« (D III, 22 and 637). Summarizing, Grundtvig can therefore formulate the aims of the folk high schools thus:

> What the high school must work on is that everyone can return to his daily task with enhanced delight, with a gaze made clear upon [i.e. an improved understanding of] the human and civic circumstances, especially in his *fatherland*, and with quickened gladsome feeling of the *people's fellowship* which makes him a participant in all the greatness and goodness which hitherto and hereafter shall be achieved by the people to which he belongs. (GSkV II, 238).

Despite considerable difference in the language used, there is in the matter itself a good accord with Freire's driving idea, both negatively and positively. They agree to work for the empowerment of the people, culturally (»gaze made clear« etc. ) socially, and politically (»a participant in all ... that shall be achieved by the people.«)

## Conscientization

The word »conscientization« or its equivalent does not, to our knowledge, occur in Grundtvig. The closest we can find to a NEGATIVE aim in this area is probably his intent, to combat »Slave-mindedness« (see above). As for the POSITIVE aim, we may say that the reality which Freire designates »conscientization« corresponds in Grundtvig's terminology to »The People gradually awakened to Self-awareness« (GSkV II, 183). »To arouse or awaken« are terms often used in Grundtvig when he wants to describe the aims of the folk high school. Best known is probably Grundtvig's reply to Peter Larsen Skræppenborg (1854), when he spoke the often quoted words:

> To awaken, nourish, and enlighten the *human life* which we dare and must presuppose in *Danish* youth, is the sole aim of the Danish folk high school... (GSkV II, 279).

Formulations close to this one are found in the third volume of the periodical »Danskeren« of 1850. Grundtvig is here able to refer to Heimdall, the champion of Danish values, as »Minister of Education in Asgard« (D III, 160, cf. GSkV II, 162-164). In Norse mythology Heimdall is the vigilant watchman who, in times of crisis, arouses the gods to action. Heimdall, therefore, fits beautifully into Grundtvig's context when he speaks of awakening the people. We can also refer to the following declaration, where the negative and the positive aims are both expressed:

> That in fact schooling, as it is normally carried on, in no way serves to awaken, nourish, strengthen, and gladden true human life, but rather to hinder, subjugate, and consume it, is not only a daily experience of the most grievous kind, but of necessity accords with that true proverb »The letter killeth...« (D III, 314).

And a little later in the same article we find the positive aim expressed in the words that life must be »awakened and implanted, nourished and developed« in the children (ib. 317). It is hard to see any objective difference between Freire's words about »conscientization« and Grundtvig's stress on awakening, nourishing, strengthening... implanting and developing.

## *Emancipation*

Freire says either »emancipation« or »freedom«, whereas Grundtvig speaks of »freedom«. The NEGATIVE aim is usually expressed by Freire with »oppression« and »disempowerment«. In his description of what he rejects, Grundtvig will often use the word »duress« for instance, and point generally to all that will »prevent, suppress and corrode« human life, see for instance the above quotation.

In POSITIVE formulations it is not only true that both Freire and Grundtvig are aware that the concept of »freedom« contains both individual and collective perspectives. They also agree that the idea of equality must be brought in if one is to the express the political aspects of the idea of freedom, see above on empowerment. For instance, Grundtvig can stress that the school he envisages should bridge the deep class divisions existing in society.

> (The purpose of the »living interaction« is that) »a bridge should be laid across the yawning chasm which hierarchy, aristocracy, Latinery, and snobbishness have entrenched between almost all the people on the one hand and its leaders and teachers with a handful of so-called »educated« and enlightened on the other. Otherwise almost all civic society and all tranquil historical development will perish in the chasm. (GSkV II, 183)

Nevertheless, right from early youth, Grundtvig felt a rooted aversion to the word »equality«, which for him expresses an illusion, »a »will-o'-the-wisp« (Bugge, 1979). Although there is justification for the cause, in his view humans are not uniform and can never become so. In his later works Grundtvig suggests several different solutions to the problem of equality. In one of his best-known songs he speaks of »*equal dignity* in castle and cottage«. He also speaks about the feeling of national solidarity, »folkeligheden«, a Danish word which can be divided into »folk« (people) and »lighed« (equality). »Folke-Lighed [he says] is a Nordic word; it gently solves the riddle of equality« (ib. p. 208). »Gently«, i.e. without the bluster and bloodshed of revolution.

A third, less-well-known solution is Grundtvig's stressing of the concept of »ligelighed« (equity). The reason for Grundtvig's preference for this word is probably that it avoids any misunderstanding of »lighed«, which in Danish can mean likeness, similarity, as well as equality. In the present context it is noteworthy that Grundtvig can make a very close link between the ideas of freedom and equity. Among all the good things that may be said about the new Constitution of 1849, in one of his articles of 1850 Grundtvig particularly emphasizes the Constitution's introduction of »human liberty and equity, which is always needed, and therefore ought never to be missing.« (D III, 331). In this article he returns several times to this pair of concepts, which for him designate »the conditions for a doughty and happy lifetime« (ib. 329). The content of the concept is defined as including the abolition of privileges and the enshrining of equal opportunities, for he points to:

> the true *equity*, which only occurs where all civic favourings, all *privileges* which do not entail answering *obligations* and sacrifices, are annulled without *compensation*, and *equal access* is opened for all citizens to any post and *activity* for which they show themselves apt. (D III, 332-333).

In conclusion, the concepts of education, freedom, and equity are placed alongside one another:

> Civic freedom is also the precondition for genuine popular and civic education, which alone can, but also assuredly will, obtain for the Danish people the civic freedom and equity which this people desires and needs. (D III, 336).

It has long been known that the concept of freedom is central to Grundtvig's world of ideas. In the present context it has proved to be of importance that it contains a combination of ideas common to both Grundtvig and Freire.

## Humanization

In Grundtvig, the element that corresponds to Freire's words about humanization, is his repeated stress on the necessity of a school for life. The life in view is human life in a context of a people (folk) and common humanity, i.e. a universal context. Thus, it is stressed that in the school:

> *Human life* must be mirrored for children and young people, must appeal, awaken, and nurture what corresponds within them, and *prepare* them thereby for *real life* in whatever setting; that is the school for life with *popular* enlightenment and education, which I wish for the whole human world (D III, 320) (Grundtvig says "Mandhjem", in Nordic mythology the part of the world inhabited by men).

It is characteristic of Grundtvig that in this way he prioritizes what belongs to the people and to all mankind, what he calls the basically human, above the needs of the individual: »What may be good and beneficial for individuals, must be left to the individuals, their own wits, their diligence, and good fortune.« (GSkV II, 253, cf. D III, 317).

It is not known whether Freire operates with similar priorities in his programme for humanization, nor whether he, like Grundtvig, looks along overlapping popular and universal lines. But it might be worth investigating! At any rate, there is agreement on one important point: the conviction of both thinkers that backward social groups have lost the urge and ability to express themselves orally. These people have become silent and passive and thus lost an essential ingredient in their humanness. It is this unhumanness, the deathly silence that both Grundtvig and Freire wish to combat.

To sum up then, we can state that the new interpretation using basic concepts from Freire takes us a long way into Grundtvig's world of ideas. Despite differences in usage, time and again we can note an affinity in the cause they have in view. This conclusion leads on to a renewed dialogue with the colleagues in Bangladesh.

## (6) New priorities

For a fresh interpretation of Grundtvig's educational ideas, it is necessary to make fresh priorities as regards their content. The new priorities arise against the background of the particular social and political, economic and cultural conditions in the country. For instance, in Bangladesh, they have chosen to construe the word »people« as a term describing the lowest groups in society (see above). This is done, because the helping of these groups is accorded a higher priority than helping the whole population as such. Furthermore, literacy is given particular priority. This is because a considerable part of the rural population is illiterate. When the folk high schools began their operations in Denmark in the mid 19th century, the Education Acts of 1814 onward meant that it was reasonable to expect that, if not all, then the majority of those who enrolled as students were able to read and write.

Finally, as we have mentioned, the gonobidyalayas give high priority to the teaching of practical skills as an important and obvious component of their idea of what a school for life is and should be. This means that an important part of teaching time is spent on teaching the students some practical skills, so that when they leave they are able to make a living. This kind of vocational training is (with a few exceptions) unknown at Danish folk high schools. This leads a Danish observer to make the justified comment:

> in Danish eyes, it can be hard to accept that a stay at a gonobidyalaya - inspired by the Danish folk high school - should be spent in learning a trade. (Skovmand Jensen, 1989).

The relationship between a general education for life on the one hand and a specialized, vocational training on the other has been a constantly recurring subject of debate in most of the history of folk high schools in Denmark (cf. Lundgaard, 1991; Birkelund, 1999). Over time, a number of schools aiming at training in a particular trade have emerged, e.g. agricultural schools, fishery schools, domestic science schools etc.

Most of these institutions have doubtless understood their own activity as being closely akin to those of the folk high schools. However, the majority of representatives of folk high schools have so far maintained that their primary task is general education. And on this point current legislation in Denmark is in accord with the majority view.

Against this background, it is intriguing that over the last 30 years or so there have been a few signs of a fresh assessment of Grundtvig's understanding of the relation between general and practical education. In Denmark this process began in a small way in 1968, when a fragment of a hitherto unknown Grundtvig manuscript of 1837-38 was published. Here, Grundtvig describes how the new school in the town of Sorø of which he dreams is surrounded by several workshops called »The Touchstone«. This expression is explained thus:

> This is what they call the new part of the town with all the workshops where the new inventions pass through purgatory and where all the young fellows who have learnt something with their hands can earn their bread while they study at the Academy and thus advance in their craft.« (GSkV II, 304).

In the early 1970s, against the background of Neo-Marxism, one or two people began to reflect upon the theory-praxis relationship in Grundtvig's thought (e.g. Larsen, 1974). Then in 1983 Dan Ch. Christensen published the whole of the 1937/38 text along with a second dialogue of the same time. Both texts stress education with a view to »practical proficiency« (GSkV I, 240). Finally we can refer to Regner Birkelund's PhD thesis of 1998 about Testrup Folk High School, which from 1927 to 1975 functioned as a high school of nursing. In Birkelund's estimation, the Testrup group with their practical orientation were far more in accord with Grundtvig's ideas than their critics thought. In the Third World Kachi Ozumba in particular has through the 1990s been defending a re-interpretation of Grundtvig's educational ideas along practical, vocational lines.

Against this background, the question arises whether the division into general and practical teaching which the gonobidyalayas maintain should not be seen as an element in this process of re-interpretation? In that connection, though, it should be noted that the same conclusion is not drawn in Bangladesh as by Ozumba at his school in Nigeria. At the gonobidyalayas, there has been only a partial not a complete change of priorities. The general education is still what takes up most of the timetable. The considerable number of lessons in practical skills has given this education a position that not only underlines its importance in the particular situation, but is also in accord with a particular trend in recent Grundtvig interpretation.

# THE COMMON AND THE PARTICULAR

*Bangladesh, Denmark, and The Third World*

For nations and human beings to know one another, conversation is required. It is also true that dialogue takes place in an interplay between things shared and things peculiar to each side. The starting-point for the conversation is that people have something in common. They must have a language which both understand, and they must have something to talk about, some matter which both have on their mind. Gradually, as dialogue has been established, they discover that a longer and less shallow acquaintance brings the insight that the other party has some special, surprising and specific characteristics.

So too in the partnership with our colleagues in Bangladesh, we have something in common. We have English as a language which both sides feel comfortable using. And we have a shared matter on our mind: that aid may be given to the third-world country of Bangladesh. We want to give this assistance, and they want to receive it.

As the years have passed, we have become aware of what is particular. Our partners in Bangladesh have discovered that Denmark may resemble the USA and other western donor countries in that our general standard of living is incredibly high, but they have also discovered that Denmark is special in that the Danes have something they call »folk high schools«, i.e. a viable tradition of adult education, and now they know that the Danes would like to help the population of Bangladesh to derive benefit and pleasure from these institutions.

It would be futile to go beyond these general remarks about how our partners in Bangladesh view us. It would entail too much guesswork. It is far more interesting for us to try to take some further steps towards learning what is special about Bangladesh. This attempt must be governed by the caveat that the following observations are of course limited by the observer's interests and source material. Others must supply the deficiencies.

Bangladesh has much in common with other developing countries. Politically, it did not achieve independence until the post-war period. Socially, the gulf between rich and poor is so profound that we in Denmark can scarcely take it in. Economically, Bangladesh is poor just as other developing countries are. A rapidly growing population means that any gain from improvements is quickly wiped out by increased demand for food and other elementary resources. Culturally, here as in other developing countries, the excessive level of illiteracy hampers progress.

But Bangladesh is also sui generis. Politically, independence was not won in a clash with a European colonial power, but through a civil war. The fact that is was necessary to liberate the population from oppression by co-religionists whom people had regarded as their true friends was - and to some extent still is - a national trauma. In comparison, the British colonial power belongs to a remote and insubstantial past and plays no important role in the self-awareness of the people of present-day Bangladesh.

Socially, although the situation in Bangladesh is serious, it is not hopeless. There are opportunities for social mobility that are much greater than in India, where Hinduism's caste system sets up important obstacles in many respects. Mobility is also greater than in many African countries, where the perpetuation of internal tribal conflicts leads to much internal oppression and misery. Bangladesh does still have the influential families as political and economic centres of power, but it is a fluid situation, where changes can come about from one day to the next. Caste systems or tribal systems cannot be changed so easily.

Culturally, Bangladesh is actually favoured. Whereas India and many African states are divided up into numerous language groups, Bangladesh has one common language. There is also a common Bengali cultural tradition, of which people are rightly proud. And as we have mentioned, internal communications are easy because of the numerous waterways. The economy remains as the country's really great and grave problem. An important prerequisite for any effective improvement of the economy is that the very considerable, untapped human resources among women, young illiterates, and the unemployed should be activated. This is where the need for adult education enters the picture. There are two questions here that urgently need answering:

- What should this adult education be about? What should *the focus* or central aim of the education be?
- What *human resources* can be counted on in the population in this context?

## *The focus of the education*

What should be the focus? In a 1993 study Holger Bernt Hansen dealt with this question in a broad third-world perspective. The cultural view, which to some extent was inspired by Erica Simon's ideas (see above), took centre stage in the first decades of development aid. The main point, it was thought, was a cultural struggle, in which the populations of the former colonial areas regained their confidence in their own national culture. A strong cultural awareness, it was said, was the indispensable foundation for political, social, and economic development. At the moment the folk high school entered the picture as a partner in the process, it was clear that on the basis of this Danish tradition the main task must be seen to be the strengthening of the cultural identity of the nations concerned, in other words their identity as a people (»folk«). For various reasons, this basic aim has been replaced over the last few decades by an interest in vocational training.

So much for the general features. But seen in this context, Bangladesh is a special case. As far as is known, at no time has the strengthening of cultural awareness , of Bengali national identity, been seen as the main task of the gonobidyalayas. It is true that general, all-round education takes up most room on the timetable. But this teaching is not viewed as an end in itself. It is seen as a prerequisite for the young school-leavers being able not only to make a living, but also to take a step along the road as human beings and members of society.

There is another important point. Bangladesh is special in that there is no need to work towards awakening and disseminating awareness of national identity. This already exists, as we have said several times, in the language and the culture. This self-awareness might well develop along exclusive lines. That is why the principals of the gonobidyalayas are much aware of the necessity of drawing the cultural tradition of the Hindu minority into the readings at the morning assembly. At the Rangunia Gonobidyalaya they are also particularly attentive to the culture of the tribal peoples.

We can sum up by saying that Bangladesh has a special character because, in the development process sketched out above, they skipped the first stage. Additionally, they have in fact got a step beyond the stage which aims one-sidedly at vocational training. In Bangladesh they seem to have arrived at the third stage: a well-balanced synthesis.

## Human resources

### Education and the will to reform

The second of the two questions concerns opportunities for continuing the gonobidyalayas in the future. As we know, Danish aid for the initiative is granted for a limited period. Is there a fund of human resources that may be drawn upon if required?

In discussing the future, we have sometimes encountered the view that any continuation of the gonobidyalaya project is shrouded in gloom. Some point to *elitist educational thinking* that has been inherited from the British colonial power. Others mention the *authoritarian* way of thinking endemic to Islam, which is the religion of the great majority. But the question is whether these evaluations have not been distorted by general observations made elsewhere and at other times. A closer look shows that Bangladesh is exceptional on this point as well. This needs explanation.

The reasons that the educational thinking of the British colonial power was marked by elitism were partly the British public-school tradition, partly the need to train clerical staff for the numerous colonial offices. However, it would be quite unreasonable to make an exclusively negative evaluation of this educational thinking. The Indian historian Amades Tripathi emphasizes the administrative initiatives from 1854 onward as marking a positive epoch, even as regards the education of the broad masses. A main aim of these efforts was indeed to disseminate »useful and practical knowledge suited to every station in life, to the great masses of the people« (Tripathi, pp. 59-60). A similar favourable assessment is found in the standard work on the history of Indian schools written by the authors Syed Nurullah & J.P.Naik. They describe the latter half of the 19th century, (1854-1902), as a period of progress within education. Five universities were founded, every province had an Education Department, secondary schooling was greatly expanded, and taxes began to be collected, earmarked for the education sector. And the two authors continue by saying that the period:

> saw a large increase in primary schools of the modern type; it witnessed significant developments in vocational education and in the education of such erstwhile backward groups as Muslims, Harijans, aboriginals and women. These advances, which by no means exhaust the whole list, indicate, that this was a period of steady educational development... (Nurullah & Naik, p. 131).

Although there were mistakes and backward steps, it should be said to the credit of the colonial power, that their philosophy of education was not too »elitist« to create hitherto unseen opportunities for backward social groups like Muslims, outcasts, tribals, and women. Also, it is relevant in the present context that particularly in Bengal, of which Bangladesh was once a part, the efforts of the colonial power in education had particularly great importance. Back at the beginning of the 19th century, a flourishing period of reform commen-

*An evening literacy lesson Here again the teaching is being given in a private home in a village.*

ced, which culminated in the latter half of the century. The calls for reform were brought about by both positive and negative inspiration from the educational efforts of the colonial power. People both appropriated what seemed valuable in the new, and concentrated on the central values in the cultural tradition handed down. Impelled by both impulses, profound social reforms were brought about within the Hindu community, and in the field of literature and poetry efforts were made that provoked admiration far beyond the borders of India.

Among the best-known names in the Bengali reform movement, besides the pioneer Ram Mohan Roy (1772-1833) were Debendranath Tagore (1817-1905), the poet's father, Keshub Chandra Sen (1838-1884), as well as Ishwarchandra Vidyasagar, the important figure we have already mentioned, who is little known in Europe.

This eventful process shows that Bengali culture has within it a very particular potential, which can be inspired and provoked into making a social, political, and cultural contribution. The human resources required to create a positive future are thus very much present.

## The importance of religion

We now come to the role of religion. As was the case with assessing the British colonial power, care must be taken not to jump to any one-sided negative conclusions. There are undeniably authoritarian features. The very word Islam means submission (Hjarpe, p. 14). But there is much more to be said. We described above how a particular, tolerant version of Islam developed in Bengal over the centuries. And as has been said, this »capacity for expanded community« is the hidden strength of Bangladesh (Ziring, p. 218).

If we take a further step and look at the importance of religion in schools and education, we find surprising initiatives here too. Before, during, and after colonial times, the Koran-teaching of the mosques gave all children of the faith the opportunity to learn to read, write, and reckon. It was to a limited extent indeed, but it was an effort that should not be undervalued. During independence, the religious leaders, for instance, by skilfully using their links with the Arab world, have managed to strengthen the position of religion in society and, thus, within the education sector.

As regards the religious leaders' attitude to the gonobidyalayas, the attitude on village level has, as we have mentioned, generally been that of critical evaluation and suspended judgement with a tendency towards gradual acceptance and co-operation. Also, in this context it should be recalled that when the gonobidyalaya project was set up, there were already local adult education initiatives functioning round and about in the villages, e.g. at Santosh (see above). Nor should Dr Rustam Ali in Uchai be overlooked. This local pioneer, who with pride recounted his pilgrimage to Mecca, had made a pioneering contribution to adult education. These examples show that it is quite possible for people to work constructively in this field even when they belong to an authoritarian religion.

However, it is not just the practical effort, but the principles of educational thinking on an Islamic basis that may surprise us. This is documented by a work published in 1993 by Professor *Shamsul Haque Shaidai* entitled »Education, Man and God.« The author is unusually well-qualified to give his opinion on education. For seven years he has been the principal of a teachers training college in Comilla, and for two years he has served as deputy education minister. The book is a collection of newspaper articles written in 1958-1969, i.e. in the period when Bangladesh was part of Pakistan. A slightly shorter version was published in 1967.

The first impression the book makes is that it is representative of the branch of educational philosophy which claims to speak for »Islamic Education.« This school of educational studies emerged prominently in the years after 1977 (Bugge 1981, p. 186-192). Negatively, this trend is characterized by a marked scepticism towards western educational thinking and practice, which it regards as destructive both personally and socially. The reason given for this is that all western thinking, including that on education, lacks religion as its foundational, uniting principle. In positive terms, this way of thinking views the aims of upbringing and education as the strengthening and continuation of the Islamic society, Umma, a religious-political unit built upon the spiritual and moral foundation of Islam. At the end of the 1970s, thoughts like these appeared in English in two conference reports published in Jeddah, Saudi Arabia, edited by Hussain & Ashraf and by al-Naquib al-Attas. The published articles from the 1960s published by Professor Shaidai show that similar ideas were around some twelve years previously.

Characteristic of Shaidai's book is its broad philosophical horizon. A large number of well-known philosophers are cited. From European antiquity the main names are Plato and Aristotle, and from recent times names like Bertrand Russell, A.N. Whitehead, and Arnold Toynbee are mentioned. The author is also familiar with existentialism. From Islamic tradition there are quotations from not only the historian and statesman *Ibn Khaldun* (d. 1406;Asmussen, pp. 243-246), but particularly the poet-philosopher Dr *Muhammed Iqbal* (1877-1938), called »the spiritual founder of Pakistan« (Asmussen, pp. 53-56). The latter is quoted on almost one page in three.

To characterize the work further, we can mention that the author's position seems to come close to the recent Islamic trend that is called *fundamentalism*. This movement differs from the rather more orthodox one called *traditionalism*, which in all areas wants an unchanged continuation of Islam's classical traditions. Fundamentalism is also conservative, but not orthodox. It is true that it wishes to keep Islam as the foundation of the life of the individual and society, but it also wishes to adapt the changed conditions to religious law. Or it may be expressed thus: the intentions of the law are to be actualized under changed conditions.

Several of Shaidai's basic ideas are apparently inspired by Muhammed Iqbal. This is true of the desire to urge his fellow believers to self-examination, so that basic values do not get lost. It is also true of the high assessment of the significant role of poetry in forming the mind, and of the view that the overriding goal of educational endeavours must be a free, harmonious personality. Furthermore, this freedom is achieved by learning how to make the right moral choices, which is done on the basis of faith. Finally, Shaidai agrees with Iqbal in conceiving western democracy as illusory; in the view of both, Islam alone represents true democracy.

Thus, Shaidai's book expresses ideas for which it is fairly easy to find parallels, both within the fundamentalist movement, and in Iqbal's works. But if we look closer, we discover some interesting details which cannot directly and immediately be traced back to these sources of inspiration. Some of these ideas actually resemble things Grundtvig said and wrote!

Like Grundtvig, Shaidai stresses how important it is for young people to be familiar with history and poetry. But there are differences. When Grundtvig emphasizes »the historical-poetical«, he does it to underline the cruciality of history and poetry for the »explanation of human life«. Human beings gain insight into life by following the tracks of their kindred in the past and present, partly by listening to the myths of the ancients, in which in symbolic picture language they expressed their understanding of life. In contrast, in Shaidai's view, the primary role of history is to be morally instructive (cf. pp. 144-145, 211), to give examples of good and evil and the educational significance of poetry is that it should train imagination and creativity.

Like Grundtvig, Shaidai emphasizes the human being's freedom as a goal of education. But to Grundtvig, this freedom is conceived as both individual and collective. It is not only the individual who must be enabled to think, believe, and speak freely; the people (»folk«) must also be trained in political thinking and acting, so that they can participate actively in the life of society. Shaidai conceives of freedom in a markedly individual and moral manner.

Finally, there may be good reason to look at the conception of the importance of faith for education and upbringing. In his educational writings of the 1830s, Grundtvig stresses that »Faith is not a school matter«, a view he also espoused in one of his addresses at Marielyst in 1856 (M 76). Faith belongs to the home and the church. Therefore, in a number of drafts in 1836, he stresses most strongly that education must not be given with any consideration for the person's destiny in eternity, in »the other life«. The task of education is solely to prepare for a living participation in »our present life« (GSkV II, 288-291). One might almost think that Grundtvig was directly taking issue with Shaidai, who indeed emphasizes that human beings live in two worlds, the present and the coming one, and that faith must therefore be the basis of education and upbringing. In relation to this conviction of his, Shaidai invokes not only Saint Augustine, but particularly the afore-mentioned Ibn Khaldun (pp. 60, 216). When Grundtvig speaks of man »belonging equally to two worlds, a visible and an invisible« (M, 74), he is distinguishing between the world of the body and the world of the spirit.

We can summarize by saying that Shaidai's book, like Bangladesh itself, is full of surprises.

## Gravity and humour

To write about humour is an activity that is counter-productive. The more one writes, the more boring it becomes. So finally, we shall show with a single example that Shaidai's book is refreshingly leavened with a good deal of subtle humour. In that respect he differs from his fundamentalist fellow believers, who are men of gravity from first to last!

Shaidai's humour is of that profound kind that causes us to reflect. As an illustration we can quote his refreshing despatch of the oft-repeated belittling of colonial schooling. It is said that the aim of this schooling was only to »produce clerks«. Shaidai agrees. That was precisely the purpose of colonial schools. But once we have decided that, then the next question arises:

> How do we account for the coming up of great men in the subcontinent of India: a host of outstanding men - political leaders of extraordinary ability, sincere social reformers, great writers, poets and philosophers, efficient administrators and selfless patriots. These are the men who made the history of which we are proud. They gave us a sense of direction. They enriched our poetry and literature. They mounted the gallows and filled the jails. In short, they made us what we are today. (p.223)

Nowadays the desire is not to produce clerks, but leaders. But, asks Shaidai, is there really a need for so many leaders? Perhaps we already have too many! What is needed is something quite different, a school for producing upright, honest and loyal members of society (p 225). It is perhaps here we find the closest agreement with Grundtvig.

# ABBREVIATIONS

ALC     —     Adult Literacy Courses

BACE     —     Bangladesh Association for Community Education

BRAC     —     Bangladesh Rehabilitation Assistance Committee

D III     —     Danskeren, et Ugeblad, samlet og udgivet af N.F.S. Grundtvig, Tredie Aargang (1850)

DLH     —     Danmarks Lærerhøjskole, i.e. The Danish University of Education

FFD     —     Foreningen for Folkehøjskoler i Danmark, i.e. The Association for Folk High Schools in Denmark.

GB     —     Gonobidyalaya, i.e. schools of the people

GSkV     —     Grundtvigs skoleverden i tekster og udkast, udg. af K.E. Bugge, Bd. I-II (1968)

M     —     N.F.S.Grundtvig: Taler paa Marielyst Højskole 1856-71, udg. af Steen Johansen (1956)

MUL     —     Mannobik Unnayon Lokkho, i.e. Human Resources Development.

NGO     —     Non Governmental Organisation.

# INTERVIEWS 1998-1999

| Name | Institution | Date of interview | Place of interview |
|---|---|---|---|
| Saif Uddin Ahmed | Khanjahania GB | 12/3-98 | Khanjahania |
| Dr. Rustam Ali | Uchai GB | 25/1 and 27/1-99 | Uchai |
| Teresa Chai | MUL Center | 24/1-99 | Nilphamari |
| Q.A. Chowdhury | Dhaka University | 20/3-98 | Dhaka |
| Mosharraf Hossain | Panchagram GB | 19/3-98 | Panchagram |
| Ahmed A. Jamal | Dhaka University | 20/3-98 | Dhaka |
| Fatema Kabir | Protiggya Parishad | 19/3-98 | Comilla |
| Dildur Mahmud | Central GB | 15/3-98 | Sonargaon |
| Tanvir Mokammel | Kino Eye Film | 20/3-98 and 24/11-99 | Dhaka Vedbæk |
| M.M. Rahman | Uchai GB | 26/1-99 | Uchai |

# BIBLIOGRAPHY

ABOUT MUL CENTER. Printed presentation leaflet. Undated but assignable to 1996/7. 4 columns. Another text, with almost the same wording but apparently slightly older and likewise of 4 columns, also exists.

ALI, M.M.: Bangladesh, IN T. Neville Postlethwaite (ed): International Encyclopedia of National Systems of Education, Second Edition (Cambridge University Press, 1995)

al-NAQUIB al-ATTAS, Syed Muhammad (ed): Aims and Objectives of Islamic Education (Bristol and Jeddah, 1979)

ASMUSSEN, Jes P.: Islam (1981)

BAAGØ, Kaj: Samsara. Tekster til hinduismen (1978)

BACE: Quarterly Progress Report. October-December 1998. Uchai Gonobidyalaya

BACE/FFD/DANIDA: Introducing (the) Gonobidyalaya Project. Pamphlet, 8 colums. Undated. Presumably from 1996/97.

BASHAM, A.L.: A Cultural History of India (Oxford 1975)

BAXTER, Craig: Bangladesh. A new Nation in an Old Setting (Boulder and London, 1984)

BAXTER, Craig & Syedur RAHMAN: Historical Dictionary of Bangladesh, Second Edition (London 1996)

BHATTACHARYA, Asoke: Empowering the Neoliterates. Relevance of Danish Folk High Schools and Co-operative Movements for Adult Education in India (Calcutta, 1994)

BIGGERS, Jeff: From the Dusty Soil. The Story of Mitraniketan (Mitraniketan, Vellanad, 1996)

BIRKELUND, Regner: Testrup Højskole 1927-1974, bd. 1-2 (DLH 1998)

BIRKELUND, Regner: Det grundtvigske og det rationalistiske oplysningsbegreb, *KVAN*, Vol. 19, Nr. 55 (1999)

BORGEN, Sven: Grundtvig og Freire, IN Grundtvig och folkupplysningen (Nordens Folkliga Akademi, 1978)

BORISH, Steve M.: The Land of the Living. The Danish Folk High Schools and Denmark's Non-Violent Path to Modernization (Blue Dolphin, Nevada City, California, 1991)

BROWN, Judith M.: Modern India. The Origins of an Asian Democracy (OUP, 1985)

BUGGE, K.E.: Skolen for livet. Studier over N.F.S. Grundtvigs pædagogiske tanker (1965)

BUGGE, K.E.: Lighed i skolen - belyst ud fra den franske revolution, Pestalozzi og Grundtvig, *Dansk Udsyn* 1979/3.

BUGGE, K.E.: Pædagogiske grundidéer (3.udg., 1981)

BUGGE, K.E.: Grundtvigs syn på folkelig dannelse, IN L. Zøllner (red.): Almen dannelse, folkelig dannelse, folkelig livsoplysning (1993)

BUGGE, K.E.: Some International Varieties of Grundtvig-Inspiration, IN L. Zøllner and A.M. Andersen (ed.): Enlightenment in an International Perspective (Vejle, 1995)

BUGGE, K.E.: Canada og Grundtvig (Vejle, 1997). English translation: Canada and Grundtvig (Vejle, 1999)

CHAI, Teresa: Mulighedernes skole, *Mission i Asien* 1998/3.

CHOWDHURY, Subrata Roy: The Genesis of Bangladesh (London, 1972)

CHRISTENSEN, Dan Ch.(udg.): N.F.S. Grundtvig. To Dialoger om Højskolen (1983)

COLLINS, Larry & Dominique LAPIERRE: Freedom at Midnight (New York, 1975)

DANISH CHURCH MISSION IN ASIA. Dansk Santalmission (1997).

DOVE, Linda: The Political Context of Education in Bangladesh 1971-80, IN Patricia Broadfoot et al. (ed.): Politics and Educational Change. An International Survey (London, 1981)

EDUCATION AND SOCIAL PROGRESS. Workshop arranged by Association for Danish Folk High Schools (FFD, 1995)

EHLERS, Søren: Ungdomsliv. Studier i folkeoplysende virksomhed for unge i Danmark 1900-1925 (2000)

EICHBERG, Henning (ed.): Schools for Life (FFD, 1992)

FINAL EVALUATION REPORT. Community School Project. Protiggya Parishad (1999)

FINAL EVALUATION STUDY of the Gonobidyalaya Project (1987). DANIDA in co-operation with The University of Dhaka.

FINAL REPORT. Mid-term review of the Gonobidyalaya Project, Bangladesh. DANIDA & COWI Consult (Dec. 1994)

FREIRE, Paulo: Pedagogy of the Oppressed (1971). Danish translation: De undertryktes pædagogik (1973)

FREIRE, Paulo: Cultural Action for Freedom (1971). Danish translation: Kulturaktion for friheden (1974)

GANDHI, Mahatma: Ishwarchandra Vidyasagar, *Indian Opinion* 16/9-1905

GEERTSEN, Uffe: Højskoler i Bangladesh? + Bangladesh - et forarmet, konservativt samfund + Hvad er en højskole i et u-land? Articles in *Højskolebladet* 1983. Cited: 1983a.

GEERTSEN, Uffe: Kan højskoleidéen bruges i Bangladesh? *Udvikling* 1983/5. cited: 1983b.

GJESING, Knud: En missionspioner. H.P. Børresens liv med særligt henblik på hans missionsvirksomhed (1961)

GRUNDTVIG, N.F.S.: *Danskeren, et Ugeblad*. Tredie Aargang (1850)

GRUNDTVIG, N.F.S.: Taler paa Marielyst Højskole 1856-71, udg. af Steen Johansen (1956)

GRUNDTVIG, N.F.S.: To Dialoger, se CHRISTENSEN (1983)

GRUNDTVIGS SKOLEVERDEN i tekster og udkast, udg. af K.E.Bugge, bd. I-II (1968)

HAMRE, Bjørn: Gonobidyalayaer i Bangladesh. Pamphlet published by FFD (Februar 1994)

HAMRE, Bjørn: Højskoledrømme mellem Grundtvig og den bangalske virkelighed, *Vartovbogen* (KS 1994)

HANSEN, Holger Bernt: Education for Life or for Livelihood? Grundtvig and the Third World Revisited, IN A.M. Allchin, S.A.J. Bradley et al.(ed): Grundtvig in International Perspective. Aarhus University Press (2000)

HANSEN, Holger Bernt: Grundtvig, Europe and The Third World. Dilemmas and Challenges, *Grundtvig-Studier*, 1993

HANSEN, Holger Bernt: Møde mellem Afrika og Grundtvigs Norden, *Den ny Verden*, 1968/5

HARBOE, Jørgen & Jørgen SØE: På pletten i 200 År. *Udvikling*, oktober 1997

HJÄRPE, Jan: Islam. Lære og livsmønster (1982)

HOLCK, Dorthe Esbjørn: Paper, IN EDUCATION AND SOCIAL PROGRESS (1995)

HOLLMANN SØRENSEN, Tage: Bangladesh i år 2, *Mission i Asien* 1998/3

HUSAIN, Syed Sajjad & Syed Ali ASHRAF: Crisis in Muslim Education (Bristol and Jeddah, 1979)

INTRODUCING UCHAI GONOBIDYALAYA. Undated pamphlet; internal criteria indicate 1995-97.

JAMAL, Ahmed A.: Key Note Paper in the Seminar on Conscientisation of the Rural Poor. Gonobidyalaya Approach. Published by BACE/FFD/DANIDA (Dhaka, 1998)

JENSEN, Henrik & Lotte FABRIN: Gonobidyalaya - fem daghøjskoler i Bangladesh (FFD, 1997)

KABIR, Fatema: A Philosophy for World Education (Undated manuscript, 7 pages)

KABIR, Fatema: Nijera Shiki's Experience of Non-Formal Adult Education and How it Relates to Social Development, Human Rights and Democracy, IN EDUCATION AND SOCIAL PROGRESS (1995)

KAZI, Serajul Haque m.fl.: Case Study Bangladesh. Contribution to a conference on Adult Education and Socio-Economic Development, International Peoples' College (Elsinore, 1986)

LARSEN, Ejvind: Grundtvig - og noget om Marx (1974)

LSAP. Literacy Situation in Asia and the Pacific. UNESCO Regional Office (Bangkok, 1984 and 1985)

LUNDGAARD, Ebbe (ed.): The Folk High School 1970-1990. Development and Conditions (FFD, 1991)

MARTINUSSEN, John: Sydasien i kort og tal (MS, 1984)

MATUBBAR, Aroj Ali: The Quest for Truth. Secular Philosophy (Dhaka, 1998)

MOKAMMEL, Tanvir: Achin Pakhi. The Unknown Bard. Synopsis of documentary film about the folk singer Lalon (Dhaka, 1996)

MOKAMMEL, Tanvir & Abdul GOFUR:..... Undated, but internal criteria suggest 1994-95.

MUKERJI, S.N.: Education of Teachers in India I-II (Delhi, Madras, 1968)

NASRIN, Taslima: Shame (Penguin Books, India, 1994)

NURULLAH, Syed & J.P. NAIK: A Student's History of Education in India (Bombay, 1970)

O'DONNELL, Charles Peter: Bangladesh. Biography of a Muslim Nation (Boulder and London, 1984)

PLOUG OLSEN, Tom & Per SCHULTZ JØRGENSEN: Pædagogisk Workshop i Noakhali Projektet (Manuskript, Oktober 1982)

OZUMBA, Kachi: Education for Life, *Grundtvig-Studier*, 1993

OZUMBA, Kachi: The Story of Social Development, Human Rights and Democracy. Before, Then and Now, IN EDUCATION AND SOCIAL PROGRESS (1995)

OZUMBA, Kachi: The Task of the Folk High School in Africa, IN EICHBERG (1992)

SADASIVAM, Bharrati: Bloody Conflict in the Name of Rama. Article translated from The Times of India, Politiken 8.12.1992.

SHAIDAI, Shamsul Haque: Education, Man and God (Dhaka, 1993)

SIMON, Erica: Réveil national et culture populaire en Scandinavie (Paris, 1960)

SKOVMAND JENSEN, Gunhild: Højskoler i Bangladesh, *Højskolebladet*, 1989

SMILLIE, Ian: Words and Deeds. BRAC at 25 (Dhaka, 1997)

SMITH, D.E.: India as a Secular State. Second Printing (Princeton, N.J. 1967)

SMITH, D.E.: Religion, Politics and Social Change in the Third World (New York, London, 1971)

STATESMAN's YEARBOOK, se TURNER, Barry

TRIPATHI, Amales: Vidyasagar. The Traditional Moderniser (Calcutta, 1998)

TURNER, Barry (ed.): The Statesman's Yearbook 2000 (London, 1999). Covers the period March 1998- March 1999.

WALKER, Benjamin: Hindu-World I-II (London, 1968)

ZIRING, Lawrence: Bangladesh. From Mujib to Ershad. An Interpretive Study (Dhaka, 1994)